TRACING YOUR JEWISH ANCESTORS

TRACING YOUR JEWISH ANCESTORS

A Guide for Family Historians

ROSEMARY WENZERUL

Pen & Sword
FAMILY HISTORY

First published in Great Britain in 2008 by
PEN & SWORD FAMILY HISTORY

an imprint of
Pen & Sword Books Ltd
47 Church Street
Barnsley
South Yorkshire
S70 2AS

ISBN 978 1 84415 788 4

A CIP catalogue record for this book is
available from the British Library.

Typeset in Ehrhardt and Optima

Printed and bound in England by
CPI UK

Pen & Sword Books Ltd incorporates the imprints of
Pen & Sword Aviation, Pen & Sword Family History, Pen & Sword Maritime, Pen
& Sword Military, Wharncliffe Local History, Pen & Sword Select, Pen & Sword
Military Classics, Leo Cooper, Remember When, Seaforth Publishing and
Frontline Publishing

For a complete list of Pen & Sword titles please contact
PEN & SWORD BOOKS LIMITED
47 Church Street, Barnsley, South Yorkshire, S70 2AS, England
E-mail: enquiries@pen-and-sword.co.uk
Website: www.pen-and-sword.co.uk

Contents

Preface vii

Introduction   A Brief Social History 1

Chapter 1   Where Do I Begin? 9

Chapter 2   Drawing Your Family Tree 19

Chapter 3   Links to the Internet 28

Chapter 4   Public Records 38

Chapter 5   Archives 52

Chapter 6   Libraries and Museums 64

Chapter 7   Marriage and Divorce 78

Chapter 8   Death and Burial 87

Chapter 9   Reading Gravestones 92

Chapter 10   Extending Your Family History 97

Chapter 11   The Armed Forces 107

Chapter 12   The Holocaust 120

Chapter 13   Names 134

Chapter 14   Medical 137

Chapter 15   Heraldry 142

Chapter 16   UK Connections 146

Chapter 17   Overseas Connections 152

Chapter 18   Case Studies 176

Glossary   181

Bibliography   184

Index   195

זְכֹר יְמוֹת עוֹלָם בִּינוּ שְׁנוֹת דֹּר וָדֹר

שְׁאַל אָבִיךָ וְיַגֵּדְךָ זְקֵנֶיךָ וְיֹאמְרוּ לָךְ :

'Remember the days of old, consider the years of many generations:
Ask thy father, and he will declare unto thee:
Thine elders, and they will tell thee.'

Deuteronomy 32:7   דברים לב ז

Preface

Welcome to the Wonderful World
of Jewish Genealogy

This book is written in an uncomplicated manner and is aimed at those readers who are just beginning to explore their family history. It will also be a valuable source of reference for readers with more experience of the subject.

Finding out about your family's history is both fascinating and extremely rewarding. It is so exciting when links are made with other genealogists, exchanging information and discovering new relations along the way. Remember, family history is not just a hobby, it is a legacy to be passed on to future generations. Therefore, make a start on your family history now, before you find that there is nobody around to help you.

With programmes such as *Who Do You Think You Are?* family history has become more popular than ever. It has prompted people to look more closely at their family history and, as a result, numerous non-Jewish researchers have now discovered that they too have Jewish roots.

Today there are many areas of research that have been made accessible to the general public, from visiting archives to surfing the net. The National Archives at Kew, which now incorporates the archives previously held at the Family Record Centre, has a wealth of genealogical information for family historians who are starting their 'journey of discovery'. As well as visiting archives, do not forget to use the facilities in your local library. The librarians can always obtain books on Jewish family history for you.

Researching your Jewish roots is not as difficult as it used to be. If you have access to the Internet, then you are halfway there. As you will see from the information in this book, there are numerous websites just waiting to be visited, which will offer an unbelievable amount of information on Jewish genealogy. Even if you do not have a computer, then the book still has a tremendous amount of information that will point you in the right direction for tracing your family history.

Some parts of this book have appeared in the 'Jewish Ancestor Series', which includes the now out-of-print *Beginner's Guide to Jewish Genealogy in Great*

Britain, originally published in 2000 by the Jewish Genealogical Society of Great Britain, but much new information has been added and other sections enlarged upon and brought up to date.

Acknowledgements

I would like to thank the following people for their valuable contributions to this publication and for copyright permission: Dr Cyril Fox for the bibliography; Rosemary Hoffman for updating the section on using public records and for allowing me to use this; Dr Anthony Joseph and the genealogist from the Society of Genealogists; Else Churchill for permission to include some paragraphs from the book *My Ancestors Were Jewish*; Harvey Kaplan for information on Jewish Genealogy in Scotland; and the Scottish Jewish Archives Centre for the photo of the interior of Garnethill Synagogue; Rosalyn Livshin for information on the holdings of the Manchester Jewish Museum; Heinz Skyte for permission to use his late wife Thea's information on the Holocaust; Martin Sugarman, assistant archivist at the Jewish Military Museum, for his permission to reproduce the chaplain's card and for his lists of military awards; François Velde for giving permission to use his article on Jewish heraldry; Dr Daniel Weinbren for information on Jewish Friendly Societies; the United States Holocaust Memorial Museum for permission to use the section on *Kindertransport*; my husband Derek Wenzerul for his help with the technical side of producing this book; and Professor Uri Yosef of VirtualYeshiva.com for the section on Cohanim.

In addition, I would like to thank Rupert Harding and his colleagues at Pen & Sword for their help and support, in particular Jon Wilkinson for his design of the outer jacket and Elizabeth Stone for copy-editing the text.

Introduction

A Brief Social History

There are stories that Jewish traders were involved with Phoenician ships in the Cornish tin trade in pre-Roman times, but the first documented references to Jews in England relate to those Jews who arrived during and after the Norman invasion as part of the retinue of William the Conqueror. They settled in various Norman administrative bases, including Lincoln and at a site in the City of London still known today as Old Jewry.

In 1190 the massacre took place of the Jews in York – this was at the site of Clifford's Tower (see photograph below).

'On the night of Friday 16 March 1190 some 150 Jews and Jewesses of York having sought protection in the Royal Castle on this site from a mob incited by Richard Malebisse and others chose to die at each other's hands rather than renounce their faith.'

ישימו לד כבוד ותהלתו באיים
'Let them give glory unto the Lord and declare His praise'
Isaiah 42:12

In 1290, Edward I expelled the Jews from England. After the expulsion of the Jews from Spain in 1492, a Marrano community was established in London. In 1656 the Spanish and Portuguese Congregation in London was openly established (Sephardic). At the end of the seventeenth century the Ashkenazi community followed.

Clifford's Tower, York.

Jewish population

In 1734, D'Blossiers Tovey put the Jewish population of England at around 6,000, and half of these at least must have been Ashkenazim. Various estimates of the Jewish population were made in 1753 at the time of the Jews' Naturalization Bill, which seemed to indicate a population of 8,000, or 1,000 households. At the end of the eighteenth century, Patrick Colquhoun estimated the total Jews in England at 20,000–26,000, of whom 15,000–20,000 were in London and the rest were mainly in the seaports. Today, the Jewish population in Great Britain and Northern Ireland totals around 297,000.

The *Jewish Year Book*, originally published in 1896, gives details of Jewish communities, including population details in the UK and abroad.

The Jewish community in mid-nineteenth century Britain

A database relating to the Jewish community in mid-nineteenth century Britain was created by Petra Laidlaw and may be viewed on *www.jgsgb.org.uk*. It covers mainly England, Wales and Scotland, with a few additions from Northern Ireland, the Channel Islands and the Isle of Man. Most of the names, but not all, are linked to the 1851 census. There are some 18,000 names, which is about half the Jewish population in Britain at that time.

For each person, the database aims to show where they were and what they were doing, decade by decade, throughout their life. A handful of entries go back to the 1750s, or even the 1740s, and another handful lived through to the 1940s, and even 1950s. Some lived only a day or two, while others lived to 100 or more.

The core information, available for most but not all entries, is where and when the person was born; who their parents were; who they married and when; who their children were and when they were born; where they were living in 1851 and their occupation in 1851. Additional information, wherever available, includes places of residence in other decades through to the 1900s; the same with their occupations; a snapshot of faith affiliation(s) across the person's lifetime; date of death, cause of death and place of burial. There are notes on, for example, published biographical sources, related people in the database, contradictory data sources and so on. Wherever possible, source references have been included with each item of data.

Arrival in London and the UK ports

The East End of London has seen the arrival of many immigrants over the years. It was estimated that between 1881 and 1905, a million Jews left Eastern Europe for the West, with 100,000 arriving in Britain. London, Hull and Grimsby were the main ports of entry. London, as the capital, obviously attracted substantial numbers of Jewish people who arrived in the port of London, many settling nearby in the area known as the East End. Conditions on board these ships were cramped and the sanitary facilities too dreadful for words. Every ship with Jewish migrants on board would be met by a representative from the Poor Jews' Temporary Shelter in London (*see 5.1.5*), which accepted only adult men. Women and children were cared for by the Jewish Association for the Protection of Girls, Women and Children. Luckily, the Shelter kept records of all who stayed there. A number of these immigrants were en route to the USA and South Africa.

Grimsby and Hull

These were two of the many east coast ports where immigrants arrived after having escaped from persecution in Eastern Europe. Many were en route to Canada and the USA but a large number stayed in the UK. This community reached its peak in the 1930s, but today there are very few Jews in these cities. Some Jews decided to move further north to the more northern and larger cities.

Most of the Jews arriving by sea came via the port of Hamburg and the other Baltic ports (*www.ancestry.com* – subscription required – for Hamburg shipping records). Those in transit to the New World would travel by train to Liverpool and onwards by sea to North America. Those who stayed as new immigrants formed a community near the docks, in the poorest part of the town.

The earliest reference to Jews in Hull is for a resident of 1766. The population grew until it reached a maximum of about 2,000 at the turn of the twentieth century. Hull has five cemeteries for the Orthodox community and one for the Reform, holding a total of 2,500 burials. The exact year when the first cemetery was acquired is unknown, but evidence suggests about 1780, the date of the opening of the first synagogue. If 1780 is correct, this makes it about the ninth oldest provincial cemetery in England.

Jews were living in Grimsby before 1290. Since Grimsby was a major UK port, large numbers of Jews landed from Eastern Europe to escape persecution. Both the synagogue and the cemetery were consecrated in 1885. Records for the Jewish community are held at the South Humberside Area Archive Office (*see 5.13*) and also at the Jewish Studies Library, University College in London.

Leeds

Jews have lived in Leeds from the middle of the eighteenth century. Jewish immigrants arrived in Leeds from Russian-controlled areas, in particular from the area that is now Lithuania and north-east Poland. Although they arrived in Hull,

Leeds was on the route they were taking to Liverpool to cross the Atlantic to the USA. In 1891 when a census was taken, there were around 8,000 Jews in Leeds. By 1905, the community numbered nearly 20,000. Today, the community is back to the 8,000 mark.

Liverpool

Liverpool is one of the oldest provincial communities. Until the middle of the nineteenth century, it was the largest provincial Jewish community in the UK. According to the Jewish Communities and Records-UK (JCR-UK) website, Sephardic Jews started the Jewish community in Liverpool around 1740. They were probably connected to the small Sephardic community that had been established in Dublin. Unfortunately, this community did not survive and a new Ashkenazi one was founded in about 1780, although little is known of its early history.

Just before this, around 1770 a new wave of settlers, mainly from Europe, worshipped in a house in Frederick Street, near the river. They also had a *mikveh*. The first Jewish burial ground in Liverpool was in Stanley Street, near the synagogue (1753–70).

Genealogical and historical records pertaining to the Jewry of Liverpool and surrounding area are in the care of the Merseyside Jewish Archives, which is part of the Liverpool Record Office (*see 6.13*). This archive holds information about the Merseyside Jewish community from the eighteenth century to the present day. The records are significant as the Liverpool community was the first organized Jewish community in the north of England, and until the mid-nineteenth century it was the largest provincial Jewish community.

Manchester

The Manchester Jewish community dates from the 1780s and today is the second largest community in the UK, with around 35,000 people and growing. In the 1870s two Sephardic communities were formed in Manchester, one in Cheetham Hill and the other in West Didsbury; the synagogue of the former is now the Manchester Jewish Museum (*see 6.23*). There are numerous Jewish cemeteries in Manchester, though unfortunately there is no central source of burial information. Each synagogue had its own burial society and buried their members in their own or jointly run Jewish cemeteries. The Central Reference Library and Archives in St. Peter's Square plus the Manchester Jewish Museum hold records.

Poor Conditions in the East End of London

In the East End of London, the Jews lived in very poor and cramped conditions, many to a small room. They settled in the streets around the Whitechapel Road area, through Houndsditch and Middlesex Street to Commercial Street.

Dutch Jews

The Dutch Jews settled in and around the Tenterground in Spitalfields (the Tenterground is named after the tenter frames used to dry and stretch woven cloth, hence the saying 'being on tenter hooks'). This was originally an area of open ground about 150 metres square, surrounded by the weavers' houses and workshops in White's Row, Wentworth Street, Bell Lane and Rose Lane (the last of which no longer exists). When the Dutch Jews settled there, the Tenterground comprised Butler, Freeman, Palmer, Tilley, Shepherd and Tenter Streets (see *www.jacobus.org.uk*).

Trades

In the 1840s, the centres for the old clothes trade were based in the Rag Fair in Rosemary Lane (which is now known as Royal Mint Street) and in the two markets off Houndsditch. Petticoat Lane market was originally founded by Huguenot lace-makers in the seventeenth century, who came to London from France to sell petticoats and lace. However, in 1830 the street was renamed Middlesex Street, as the Victorians wanted to avoid mention of ladies' underwear. The adjoining streets were alive with all sorts of Jewish traders and street traders selling their wares.

During the 1850s all kinds of businesses and business people emerged, from the very wealthy – stockbrokers and merchant bankers – to the middle classes – manufacturers of umbrellas and walking sticks, wholesalers and importers of oranges, lemons, nuts and so forth – and finally the smaller manufacturers and retailers, who were classed as general dealers, and who set up businesses in back rooms, sheds and improvised workshops. The majority of smaller manufacturers were tailors although others were in the boot and shoe trades and in the tobacco trade. The tobacco trade was mainly associated with Dutch Jews.

There were also Jewish bakers, for example from about 1700 Jewish Passover cake (*Matza*) bakers (see *www.lizlo.com/passovercakebakers.htm*).

The emancipation of the Jews in England

According to Dr Anthony Joseph, numerous professions were closed to Jews and many schools applied restrictions until late into the nineteenth century. Land ownership was similarly a difficulty, although the collection of local taxes, including rates, was applied to whichever person or persons were living in a property. In the seventeenth and eighteenth centuries, Jews were excluded from the Freedom of the City of London (which caused difficulty for retailing) but many Jews did join the City Livery Companies. A surprising number of Jews availed themselves of insurance facilities, and the lists of policy holders from the eighteenth-century insurance companies, held at the Guildhall Library (*see 6.4*), can be a very fruitful genealogical source.

In general terms, the state viewed the Jewish community as autonomous and self-regulating, so its dealings with the community tended to be via such quasi-representative organizations as the Board of Deputies (established in 1760). Jews (and Quakers) were exempted from the provisions of the Hardwicke Marriage Act of 1753, which otherwise required all marriages solemnized in England and Wales to be conducted through the authority of a clergyman. The Hardwicke exemption also allowed Jewish marriages to be solemnized anywhere in the country (and not specifically in a licensed building for the purpose), a privilege which the rest of British society has only acquired in the past few years.

Synagogues

Each wave of immigrants left their mark on the East End of London, for instance, the Jamme Masjid or Great London Mosque (founded in 1976 – *see photograph below*) currently on the corner of Fournier Street and Brick Lane, was originally a Huguenot church, built in 1743 by Huguenot refugees fleeing persecution in France. In 1809 the building was used by Methodists. In the late nineteenth century, when Jewish immigrants arrived, it was turned into the Spitalfields Great Synagogue (Machzike Adass Synagogue) and was used by the Orthodox Jewish community.

In 1887 Samuel Montagu noticed that there were a number of individual synagogues in the area and amalgamated them together to form the Federation of Synagogues. Very few of these early synagogues still exist. The famous Bevis Marks Synagogue (Sephardic), tucked away in a very small courtyard, was built for the Spanish and Portuguese Jewish community in 1701, replacing the original synagogue dating from 1656

The Jamme Masjid or Great London Mosque. housed on the upper floor of a building in Creechurch Lane. Bevis Marks Synagogue was modelled on the Portuguese synagogue in Amsterdam. It has a beautiful interior with its magnificent brass candelabra and the finest collection of Cromwellian and Queen Anne furniture in the country.

Schools

During the 1850s, the Jewish community in London and the main provincial towns had a number of voluntary day schools. These taught English, arithmetic, history and geography as well as Hebrew and Jewish studies. Off Petticoat Lane (which is now known as Middlesex Street) was Bell Lane, where the famous Jews' Free School (JFS) was sited. This was founded in 1732. At the end of the nineteenth century the JFS had over 4,000 pupils, making it the largest school in Europe.

Redevelopment of the area

Unfortunately, today much of the area has disappeared due to bombing during the Second World War, redevelopment of the area and, in addition, some of the streets have been renamed. Some of the famous shops and markets in the area, such as Bloom's kosher restaurant with its wonderful hot salt beef, no longer exist. Bloom's opened in the 1920s in Brick Lane and by the 1950s had premises in Whitechapel High Street. Petticoat Lane market, which was once alive with Jewish traders, has now been taken over by the new community in the area.

If your ancestors lived in the East End, taking a walk on a sunny day 'on the streets where they lived' can be a very nostalgic experience. Even if some of the buildings you are looking for are no longer there, you will find that most of the street names have still survived – so let your imagination do the rest!

East End walks

If you are going on one of these walks, try to find one which visits Bevis Marks Synagogue (Sephardi), which is over 300 years old, and Sandys Row Synagogue, established in 1854 and the oldest Ashkenazi synagogue in London. They are well worth a visit. There is usually a small charge for these tours, especially if you have one of the Blue Badge Guides. Both these

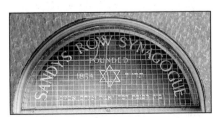

Glass section over main door of Sandys Row Synagogue.

synagogues hold services – please check service times before visiting them. Only four synagogues in the area now survive.

JEWISH EAST END CELEBRATION SOCIETY
85–87 Bayham Street, London NW1 OAG
Guide: Clive Bettington
E-mail: c.bettington@jeecs.org.uk or enquiries@jeecs.org.uk
Website: *www.jeecs.org.uk*

The Society aims to focus attention on Jewish life and culture in the East End of London. It organizes walks, talks and events in and pertaining to the Jewish East End; identifies buildings and organizations in danger of sale or neglect; creates, publishes and distributes a newsletter about the Jewish East End; publishes details of Jewish walks and the Jewish history in the area; encourages blue plaques to be erected at appropriate sites; compiles a list of literary works with reference to the Jewish East End.

BLUE PLAQUES

The blue plaques scheme is run by English Heritage in London. On your walks, always look out for and read these plaques which are on so many of the buildings in this area – a number are of Jewish interest. These will show who lived at a particular address: for example, Israel Zangwill lived at 288 Old Ford Road, Bethnal Green, London, E2. His plaque says 'Israel Zangwill 1864–1926, writer and philanthropist lived here'. Some plaques just commemorate an anniversary, for example the 130th anniversary of the Board of Guardians.

OLD LONDON MAPS

The website *www.victorianlondon.org/frame-maps.htm* has several maps of London from 1827–99. In addition it holds a lot of information about the Victorian era. (*See also 10.1.10*)

> **Further reading**
> Gerry Black, *The History of the Jews' Free School since 1732* (Tymsder Publishing, 1998).
>
> Peter Renton, *The Lost Synagogues of London* (Tymsder Publishing 2000).

Chapter 1

WHERE DO I BEGIN?

It is important to understand where your Jewish genealogical roots began. The lineage of the Patriarchs from Adam to Joseph is given in the first book of the bible, the Book of Genesis. It gives details of their ages and first born. The scripture is quite specific as to the ages involved.

Twelve Tribes of Israel

Jacob fathered twelve sons, namely, Asher (אשר), Benjamin (בנימין), Dan (דן), Gad (גד), Issachar (יששכר), Joseph (יוסף), Judah (יהודה), Levi (לוי), Naphtali (נפתלי), Reuben (ראובן), Simeon (שמעון) and Zebulun (זבולן). They are the ancestors of the tribes of Israel, and the ones for whom the tribes are named. Each occupied a separate territory (except for the tribe of Levi, which was set apart to serve in the Holy Temple).

There are three types of Jews, Yisrael, Levi and Cohen.

• Yisrael refers to a Jew who is neither a Levi nor a Cohen.
• Levites are the descendants of Jacob's son Levi and his tribe; historically, Levites served as assistants to the Temple priests.
• Cohanim are the direct descendants from Moses' brother Aaron, the first priest; historically, Cohanim served as the Temple priests.

Today a Jew is recognized as a Cohen if he is a descendant of Aaron from the Levi tribe. Cohanim maintain a number of privileges and obligations within the Jewish religion. They recite the 'priestly blessing' during some synagogue services, they are the first to be called up (*aliyah*) to read from the *Sefer Torah* (ספר תורה). Orthodox Cohanim still observe prohibitions such as not marrying a divorced woman or a convert and not coming into contact with the dead (see Chapter 9, which shows the gravestone symbols for Cohanim and Levites).

According to Jewish law, lineage is passed from the biological father (e.g.

Numbers 1:8), while the identity as a Jew is passed by the mother (Deuteronomy 7:3–4; Ezra 10:2–3). In this fashion, the priestly lineage is identified and has, therefore, been preserved through history.

On the eighth day following the birth of a son whose father is a Cohen, as part of the circumcision ritual the child is also given a name to which is appended the Hebrew title *ha'cohen* (the same applies to a son whose father is a Levite, though in this case the Hebrew name is appended with the Hebrew title *ha'levi*).

GENEALOGY
The fact that genealogies are listed in the Old Testament indicates that they had, and still have, a place in Judaism. It is important to note that the Tribe of Levi was particularly important since the lines of the Cohanim and Levites had to be kept pure (Exodus 40:15; Numbers 25:12–13 and Ezra 2:61–2).[1]

GEOGRAPHICAL SPLITS
In addition to the three types of Jewish people mentioned above, there are also geographical splits. Jews who originally came from the Spanish peninsula are known as Sephardic and those who lived in Northern European countries such as Poland, Lithuania and Germany were known as Ashkenazi. Each group of people has different cultures and traditions both in the home and in the synagogue.

Now you understand your basic roots, it is time to begin.

What is family history?

Family history is not just a hobby; it is a legacy to be passed on to future generations. Therefore, it is in your hands to do your best to record accurate information.

Family history is about:

• The lives of every member of your family from birth to death
• The disappointments and the joys of their life
• The characters who stood out in your family
• The family stories, recipes, remedies, holidays, customs
• The places you lived, the homes, streets, and neighbours
• Comparisons – today and many years ago.

All the above suggestions will enhance your family history, so ensure you keep them in mind when interviewing your relatives.

Before you begin any family history research, try to find out whether anyone in your family has previously produced a family tree. This will save a lot of time and effort if they have.

1.1 Collecting information – where should I begin?

There are a number of directions to follow when you are starting your family history.

- ask as many questions as possible from your family, starting with the eldest member and working downwards
- be as accurate as possible
- browse the Internet and websites relating to Jewish genealogy
- join the Jewish Genealogical Society of Great Britain
- involve yourself in discussion groups or special interest groups
- visit your local library – ask for books on Jewish genealogy
- visit archives and record offices
- look at the relevant census
- look at birth, marriage and death certificates
- look at wills.

It is essential to write down everything you know about your family (create an index or fact sheet). Keep it simple to start with. Begin, as I have said above, with the eldest member of your family, which would normally be your grandparents, or if you are lucky enough to have great-grandparents, begin with them. Fill in as much information as you can, then ask if they can complete the remaining gaps. If this is not possible, try contacting close relatives to help you. Remember, every person has a story to tell.

Do not forget to check the details of stepchildren, as children from a second marriage sometimes use different surnames.

If you have not yet invested in any family history software programme, then begin by allocating an index card (or piece of paper) for each person and write against each the information you wish to collect. As you will see from the sample card below, try to cross-reference the family members. This will make life a lot easier if you wish to transfer this information at some time in the future onto a family history computer programme. However, if you have an existing programme in place, then the data may be entered directly onto the specific screens.

These cards are easy to produce. Just type out the details four times on an A4 piece of paper, which can act as a template, then scan or photocopy these onto card as and when required. Obviously you will need to cut them into four.

NAME: GOLDSTON Isaac   INDEX CARD NUMBER: 78

	DATE	PLACE
Birth	5 April 1873	1 Sandys Row, Bishopsgate, London, E
Marriage	10 August 1897	Great Synagogue, Dukes Place, London, E
Death	20 May 1947	Paddington District (Vol.5a, Page 138)
Buried	Sec. SX. Row 5. Grave 7	Willesden Cemetery, Beaconsfield Road
RELATIVES	NAME	INDEX CARD No.
Father	Abraham Goldston	59
Mother	Amelia nee Levy	113
Spouse	Rose nee Barnett	28
Children	Alfred Goldston	79
	Agnes Goldston	80
	Leonard Goldston	81
	Marjory Goldston	82
REFERENCE	OTHER INFORMATION	INFORMATION UP-DATED
Cousin John Bluestone	Isaac was Secretary/Minister/Reader at the New West End Synagogue from 1918 – 1946	Updated 29 May 1999 Updated 14 July 2003 Updated 15 January 2007

Example of index card.

1.1.1 Fact sheet

Remember to date and record the source of your information – for example, you may be in a room with a lot of the family and they are all giving you various pieces of information. If you don't write this down at the time, then when you get home you may not remember who gave you which piece of information. In addition, you may wish to contact that particular person in the future and it is so annoying when you cannot remember who supplied the information in the first place. This also applies to reference numbers of documents or microfilm and where the sources were originally found.

On the reverse of the index card, write down any information you have about the person. By doing this it will be easy for you to compare information.

1.2 Objectives

It is now time to look at what information you have collected and then decide what information you still need to collect.

You will have four grandparents, so make a card up for each: see the above example. Using the information on each index card, generate a pedigree chart.

This will contain information about your immediate family – parents, grandparents and great-grandparents – it will not show any other relatives, such as siblings or cousins or your own children, who may be added at a later date.

1.3 Keeping accurate records

Always keep accurate records. If you are not sure of something, record it but put a note next to it saying that it has not been verified. This is important since the smallest piece of information which has been given to you, although not verified, may turn out at a later stage in your research to be extremely valuable and may point you in new directions.

With regard to using the Internet, remember that millions of people access material from this source and the material is then recirculated without checking for accuracy. Whatever you do, don't take this information at face value – it must always be verified.

1.4 How do I verify my information?

The most secure way to do this is to obtain legal or official papers. For example, if you have a 'full' as opposed to a 'short' copy of a birth certificate, this will not only verify the date of birth of the person concerned but will tell you the place of birth, their full name, sex, father's name, mother's name (including maiden name), father's occupation, the address of the informant and the date registered. Once you know when the person was born, you can then check to see whether the marriage and death certificates are accurate. Ladies sometimes put the incorrect age on their marriage certificates.

Should you have an address for a person, if you check the census returns this will verify when they were living at a particular address.

1.5 Thirty suggested questions

1.   Has anyone in your family produced a family tree? If so who?
2.   Where did the family originate from?
3.   If your relative came from abroad, how did he/she travel to England?
4.   What was the town you came from like?

5. Did your grandparents live in the same place?
6. What were your occupations/positions held?
7. How did you meet your spouse?
8. Tell me about your parents/grandparents: what language did they speak?
9. Tell me about your siblings.
10. What was your life like as a child (including the sweets you enjoyed; the games you played; your friends; club and organizations you belonged to, etc.)?
11. What were your hobbies? Did you belong to any youth movements such as the Guides, Scouts or Jewish Lads and Girls Brigade?
12. At what age did you leave school? Which school?
13. Describe your home when you were a child.
14. What did you do during the Second World War? Were you in the forces, land army, ARP or other? Where were you stationed?
15. Were you evacuated? If so, what was it like? Where were you sent? What was the family you stayed with like? What school did you attend?
16. Were any of the rest of your family in the forces? Do you have their regimental details or army record?
17. Were they on active service? If yes, where did they serve?
18. Do you have any interesting stories they told you about their time in the forces?
19. Do you own a family Bible or prayer book?
20. Do you have any old photo albums?
21. Do you have copies of any birth, marriage/*Ketubot* or death certificates?
22. Do you have any family stories or specific family phrases that have been passed down to you?
23. What would you change if you could live your life again?
24. What diseases or conditions, if any, have affected your family? (e.g. colour blindness, heart disease, diabetes.)
25. Did you have holidays as a child/adult? Where did you go?
26. Was your family religious?
27. What synagogue did you belong to /get married in?
28. Do you have any family recipes that have been handed down to you?
29. What are your happiest/unhappiest memories?
30. Have you kept any memorabilia? (e.g. Valentine cards, birthday cards, anniversary cards; wedding, Bar Mitzvah/Bat Mitzvah invitations; certificates; menus; membership cards.)

1.6 Research at home

1.6.1 Family documents

If you collect as many family documents as possible and extract all the information from them, this is an excellent way to enlarge upon your research and to preserve the material for future generations. You may find that your family have important papers, for example, naturalization papers, birth, marriage and death certificates. Because these documents include information about more than one generation of a family, access to these papers is extremely important in order to extend your research beyond the immediate members of your family.

1.6.2 Family photographs and postcards

In order to bring your family history to life, try to include as many photographs of your family as possible (*see 10.1.17*). Here are some suggestions:

Family as children.

- as children
- as adults
- weddings
- in uniform
- family graves.

AS CHILDREN
Find out the names of the children, the date and where the photograph was taken, for example at school, on holiday, etc.

The same family as adults.

As adults

Again, it is important to find out the names of the people in the photograph and where and when the photograph was taken. If possible, try to get photographs of the people as children and again as adults.

Weddings

There are numerous photographs you can take at a wedding. However, ensure you make a note of where the pictures were taken – in synagogue, at the reception, on honeymoon and so forth. Do not forget to record the date and the names of the people in the photograph and how they are related to you.

In uniform

Whether you have family who were in the Scouts or Guides or whether they were in the armed forces, photographs should be kept because every photograph conveys part of a person's life and tells a story. As above, if you have a photograph of your family when they were in the forces and also now, it's a good idea to show them together (*see 11.12 for an example*). Remember to record the person's name, regiment, service number, place and the date the photograph was taken.

Family graves

Always check with the office staff of the cemetery before taking photographs. You will need to record the name of the person, their Hebrew name, date of death and Hebrew date of death, the name of the cemetery, section, row and grave number.

Postcards

Always check both sides of old postcards. In bygone days, the photograph on the postcard was of a family member. There may well be a clue to this effect on the reverse. Have a look at the date stamp on the card as this will give you an indication of the date the photograph was taken. If there is no date stamp, you may be able to date it by the costume they are wearing or by checking a Stanley Gibbons stamp catalogue for the actual stamp on the postcard.

1.7 Join a Jewish family history society

Without doubt, joining a family history society will help you to trace your family history. Most societies will arrange meetings where you can ask questions or exchange information with other like-minded people and learn new skills. The societies all produce journals or newsletters which include a wealth of information from the members. At family history society meetings there is always someone who can help you, or if not, they will know somebody who can, so it is an absolute must to join.

JEWISH GENEALOGICAL SOCIETY OF GREAT BRITAIN (JGSGB)
Library and Resource Centre
33 Seymour Place, London, W1H 5AP
E-mail: enquiries@jgsgb.org.uk
Website: *www.jgsgb.org.uk*

The JGSGB is the leading society for Jewish genealogy in Great Britain and has over 1,000 members. It encourages research and promotes the preservation of Jewish records and resources, sharing information amongst its members. See their website for details of regional groups.

Membership Enquiries
The Membership Secretary, PO Box 42780, London, N2 0YH
E-mail: membership@jgsgb.org.uk

The Members' Genealogical Resource Library contains extensive information and genealogical resources including several hundred reference books, computers and a selection of genealogical CD-ROMs and other genealogical databases. Helpers are on hand to assist. It also houses a large collection of maps and leaflets as well as microfilms and microfiches (including copies of many of the major Anglo-Jewish genealogy collections). The members' library has one of the largest collections of *Yizkor* (memorial) books in the UK. (For opening times contact the Society.) A list of books and resources is available online at *www.jgsgb.org.uk/download/ LibraryList.pdf*

The Society's publications may be viewed and ordered from their website or by e-mail request:

Shemot, *the journal of the Jewish Genealogical Society of Great Britain.* (Jewish Genealogy Society of Great Britain; photograph © Louise Messik)

JGSGB Publications, PO Box 2188, Ilford, Essex, IG1 9RE
E-mail: publications@jgsgb.org.uk
Website: *www.jgsgb.org.uk/shopping.shtml*

Shemot is the journal of the Jewish Genealogical Society of Great Britain. The JGSGB website contains a complete list of articles. It is published quarterly and is free to members of the Society.

For individual copies of any issue of *Shemot*, see the contact points above.

Note
1 Text from 'There are three types of Jews' to 'Ezra 2: 61–2' – excerpt Copyright © 2007, Prof. Uri Yosef, VirtualYeshiva.com, Messiah Truth Project, Inc. Used by permission.

Chapter 2

DRAWING YOUR FAMILY TREE

O nce you have sufficient information, it is time to prepare your family tree. This requires extreme accuracy and patience as it is usually only after several attempts that you will eventually succeed! As you will see from the following examples, there are many ways in which trees may take form. The style of your tree will be entirely up to you. The examples shown on the following pages are all correct. If you feel you are unable to draw one then you can purchase some very attractive printed ones. Adverts for these are in most genealogical magazines or may be obtained from the Society of Genealogists. Alternatively, most genealogical software packages (e.g. Brother's Keeper or Family Tree Maker) will do this too.

2.1 Drawing your tree by hand

This may be the simplest answer if you only have two or three generations to write down, but the further back and wider you go, the more awkward it will become. You will probably need a piece of paper or graph paper which will be large enough to include four generations.

Always use a pencil to write in the names so you can then erase them and replace them with the correct entry in ink. Remember to write the name of the family on the top of the sheet and the date it was compiled, for example, descendants of Jacob Vandermolen, 2 July 1998.

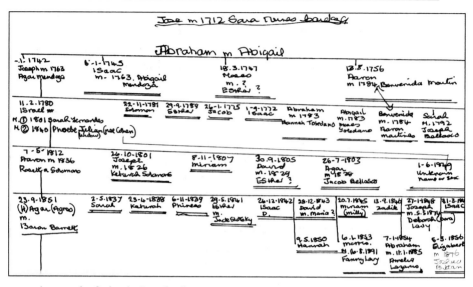

An example of a handwritten family tree.

2.1.1 What should I include?

Ideally you need to include the person's full name (women should always be listed by their maiden surname), date and place of birth, date and place of marriage and date and place of death. If you have the person's Hebrew dates which correspond to the Gregorian dates, these may be added too. To convert from a Gregorian date to a Hebrew date see *www.hebcal.com*). This obviously depends on the amount of information available. If you have not got all this information, it should not deter you from starting your tree by filling in all the names; you can always add information to it at a later date. All dates should be recorded in full, for example, 21 March 1881 (in order to avoid confusion with the way American dates are recorded), or if you are unsure of the exact year it may be shown as c.1881 (c=circa).

If a person has more than one first name, always record them all because sometimes the person concerned decides to use one of these names instead of the first name he/she was originally given. Children are usually shown left to right with the eldest child being shown on the left. Therefore, begin with yourself and work backwards. Once you have finished your paternal line, it is usual to start on your maternal line.

The above is a start. You will find that once you have completed the tree as far as you can, you will probably wish to enlarge on it. There is no rush to do this as genealogy is an ongoing interest and you can pick up where you left off at any time in the future.

I cannot stress enough how important it is to be as accurate and methodical as possible with the information you record and to try to keep your tree up to date for future generations.

2.1.2 The importance of dates

All dates are of great importance to the family historian. As well as birth, marriage and death dates, try to include as many other dates as possible, but ensure the dates are accurate – never guess them. The dates should reflect important occasions in your life. The following are just some examples:

- when you started and left your school, college or university
- when you started and left a place of employment
- if you joined the armed forces, record the date of enlistment and dates where you served and eventually when you were demobbed
- record dates of where you lived and when you moved address.

By recording these dates and any others you feel would be of importance (with as much information as possible about the places concerned), it will help future generations to track your life should they wish to do so. If they know you were at such and such a school between certain dates, they can contact the school and obtain further information. If they know the dates you lived at a certain address they can look on the census returns to see who else lived at the same address.

2.2 What type of tree should I use?

This depends on how you would like your family tree to look. Handwritten trees can quickly become a mess, as the example on the previous page shows.

2.2.1 Printed trees

If you are not artistic or feel it is too much trouble to write your family tree from scratch, the Society of Genealogists sell ready-to-fill-in trees in different sizes and you have only to fill in the details. Unfortunately, these charts limit you to recording a specified number of generations.

As you will see from the following three examples of family tree charts, there are many ways of drawing a family tree. It depends what you want out of it.

TREE CHART

The tree chart below accommodates the lateral links much more economically in space terms, but it is less easy to read at a glance than the box chart.

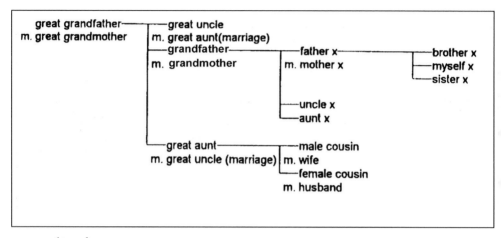

A tree chart.

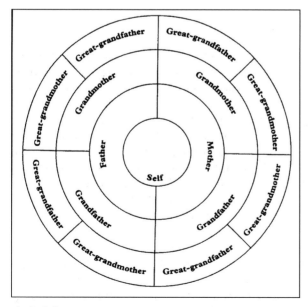

A wheel chart.

WHEEL CHART

The wheel chart is a very commercial way of displaying one person's direct ancestry, but it will not show their brothers or sisters, aunts, uncles or cousins.

BOX CHART

The box chart is a good way of showing all these lateral links, but you can soon run out of space.

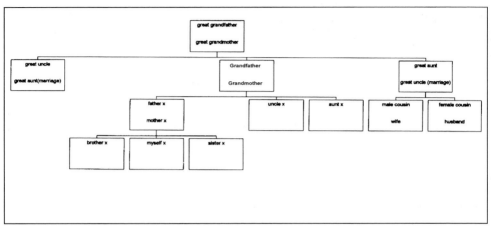

A box chart.

2.2.2 Computerized trees

It is far easier to use a computer for drawing your family tree, since you can store information on numerous generations and then print them out. There are many family tree software packages on the market, for example, Brother's Keeper, Family Tree Maker, Roots, DoroTree *(see below)* and many more. You will find a selection of genealogical software demonstrated at family history fairs, adverts and reviews in genealogical magazines such as *Family Tree Magazine, Family History Monthly, Your Family Tree*. Before deciding on any software, it is well worth looking round to see what is on the market and how prices compare.

Once you have acquired the package you feel will suit your needs, then it is time to start entering all the details of your family. One usually enters the oldest person first, followed by their children and so on.

DOROTREE

DoroTree is the perfect tool for building a Jewish family tree. It allows you to enter and print trees in both Latin and Hebrew characters without Hebrew Windows and is packed with extra features for the Jewish genealogist, including Hebrew date and name converters, *Yahrzeit* table converter, Bar/Bat Mitzvah calculator and much more.

DoroTree offers easy ways for recording and updating your data. It features optional Hebrew–English data fields, English–Hebrew first name translator, a speed search index of your family, multimedia support, a special Holocaust symbol, and handy information tabs. DoroTree is the only Jewish genealogy software programme that allows you to customize your interface by choosing from five available languages: English, Hebrew, French, Spanish, and Portuguese.

DoroTree is GEDCOM-compatible, enabling you to convey or import genealogical data from users of other genealogy software programmes. It is a little more expensive than the cheaper non-Jewish programmes but is the only software adapted specifically for the Jewish market.

The screen example below is from DoroTree – most genealogical programmes will have similar information.

Photographs may be added to your trees as the examples on the next page show. These will help bring your tree to life and will identify the members of your family for future generations.

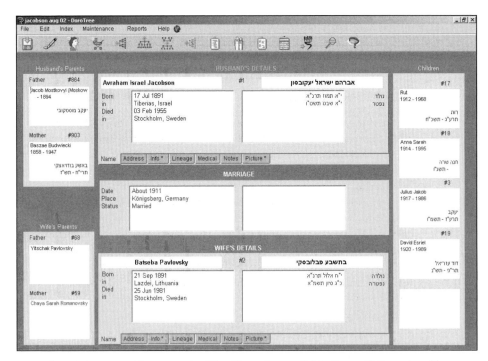

A computer screen with an example of DoroTree software. (Main Screen © Reproduced by kind permission of DoroTree)

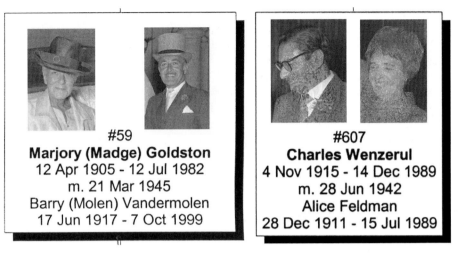

#59
Marjory (Madge) Goldston
12 Apr 1905 - 12 Jul 1982
m. 21 Mar 1945
Barry (Molen) Vandermolen
17 Jun 1917 - 7 Oct 1999

#607
Charles Wenzerul
4 Nov 1915 - 14 Dec 1989
m. 28 Jun 1942
Alice Feldman
28 Dec 1911 - 15 Jul 1989

Examples taken from Brother's Keeper programme. (© Brother's Keeper)

There are many more options available within these genealogical programmes that will help you put your family history into some sort of order.

2.2.3 Genealogical forms

The two main forms you will use in genealogical work will be the family group sheet and the pedigree chart. They may have different appearances or formats, but each has its own purpose.

The family group sheet records all known information about a single family unit. It shows the husband, wife and children. Family group sheets appear in numerous sizes and shapes, but their function remains the same, that is, to record one family group.

The pedigree chart starts with yourself and will show your direct line (blood line) of parents, grandparents, great-grandparents, and so forth. These may look like wheel charts or fan charts. No matter how they look or whether they are called pedigree charts, fan charts or wheel charts, they are basically all the same. They show your direct line.

You may wish to:

•   list the members of the family by surname
•   find all the entries for a certain location
•   carry out a word search

- find family birthdays and anniversaries
- produce family group sheets
- compute relationships
- produce statistics.

All this and much more is possible, plus the fact the information will be produced very quickly through installing a genealogical software programme that will help to organize the data you have collected.

2.3 Relationship chart

The relationship chart on the opposite page is extremely useful because it will help determine the relationship between yourself and another relative.

2.3.1 How to use the chart

1. Determine the common ancestor you and the other person share.
2. Starting with your common ancestors in the upper left corner, find yourself across the top and note the column.
3. Again, starting with your common ancestors in the upper left corner, find the other person down the left hand side of the chart and note the row.
4. Go to the box where your column and their row intersect.
5. This is the relationship you share with the other person.

For example: you are the grandson or granddaughter of the person concerned. Therefore locate this entry along the top of the chart (#3). The other person is the great-grandson or great-granddaughter of this person. Find this entry on the left hand side of the chart (#4). If you then follow the column down from (#3) and across from (#4) you will come to the relationship you share with the other person which is first cousin once removed.

Note: the diagonal highlighted boxes show persons of the same generation. The word 'removed' indicates that the two persons selected are not of the same generation.

	1	2	3	4	5	6	7	8	9	10
1	Common Ancestor	Son or Daughter	Grandson or Daughter	Great Grandson or Daughter	2nd Great Grandson or Daughter	3rd Great Grandson or Daughter	4th Great Grandson or Daughter	5th Great Grandson or Daughter	6th Great Grandson or Daughter	7th Great Grandson or Daughter
2	Son or Daughter	**Siblings (Brother or Sister)**	Nephew or Niece	Grand Nephew or Niece	Great Grand Nephew or Niece	2nd Great Grand Nephew or Niece	3rd Great Grand Nephew or Niece	4th Great Grand Nephew or Niece	5th Great Grand Nephew or Niece	6th Great Grand Nephew or Niece
3	Grandson or Daughter	Nephew or Niece	**First Cousin**	First Cousin Once Removed	First Cousin Twice Removed	First Cousin Three Times Removed	First Cousin Four Times Removed	First Cousin Five Times Removed	First Cousin Six Times Removed	First Cousin Seven Times Removed
4	Great Grandson or Daughter	Grand Nephew or Niece	First Cousin Once Removed	**Second Cousin**	Second Cousin Once Removed	Second Cousin Twice Removed	Second Cousin Three Times Removed	Second Cousin Four Times Removed	Second Cousin Five Times Removed	Second Cousin Six Times Removed
5	2nd Great Grandson or Daughter	Great Grand Nephew or Niece	First Cousin Twice Removed	Second Cousin Once Removed	**Third Cousin**	Third Cousin Once Removed	Third Cousin Twice Removed	Third Cousin Three Times Removed	Third Cousin Four Times Removed	Second Cousin Five Times Removed
6	3rd Great Grandson or Daughter	2nd Great Grand Nephew or Niece	First Cousin Three Times Removed	Second Cousin Twice Removed	Third Cousin Once Removed	**Fourth Cousin**	Fourth Cousin Once Removed	Fourth Cousin Twice Removed	Fourth Cousin Three Times Removed	Fourth Cousin Four Times Removed
7	4th Great Grandson or Daughter	3rd Great Grand Nephew or Niece	First Cousin Four Times Removed	Second Cousin Three Times Removed	Third Cousin Twice Removed	Fourth Cousin Once Removed	**Fifth Cousin**	Fifth Cousin Once Removed	Fifth Cousin Twice Removed	Fifth Cousin Three Times Removed
8	5th Great Grandson or Daughter	4th Great Grand Nephew or Niece	First Cousin Five Times Removed	Second Cousin Four Times Removed	Third Cousin Three Times Removed	Fourth Cousin Twice Removed	Fifth Cousin Once Removed	**Sixth Cousin**	Sixth Cousin Once Removed	Sixth Cousin Twice Removed
9	6th Great Grandson or Daughter	5th Great Grand Nephew or Niece	First Cousin Six Times Removed	Second Cousin Five Times Removed	Third Cousin Four Times Removed	Fourth Cousin Three Times Removed	Fifth Cousin Twice Removed	Sixth Cousin Once Removed	**Seventh Cousin**	Seventh Cousin Once Removed
10	7th Great Grandson or Daughter	6th Great Grand Nephew or Niece	First Cousin Seven Times Removed	Second Cousin Six Times Removed	Third Cousin Five Times Removed	Fourth Cousin Four Times Removed	Fifth Cousin Three Times Removed	Sixth Cousin Twice Removed	Seventh Cousin Once Removed	**Eighth Cousin**

A relationship chart. (Reproduced with the consent of © CousinCouples.com)

Chapter 3

LINKS TO THE INTERNET

nyone beginning their family history will, no doubt, want to gather as much information as possible. If you find it difficult travelling to archives and record offices but have access to the Internet, you will be able to carry out a tremendous amount of your research from home. If you do not have a computer, you can always book 'computer time' at your local library where there will be librarians available should you require assistance.

In recent years, the Internet has become one of our most useful tools. It offers much in the way of making contact with other family historians and exchanging information, or you can just surf the net to locate suitable genealogical websites with Jewish connections. Practically all the family history websites will have links pointing elsewhere. It is always sensible to have a look at these as they may lead you to additional areas of research. This chapter lists websites of particular interest to those who are researching their Jewish roots.

3.1 Where to begin

I would personally begin with JewishGen as this website is just packed with information:

3.1.1 JewishGen

www.jewishgen.org

This website covers Jewish genealogy throughout the world. There are numerous resources available on the site's home page, including the JewishGen Family Finder (a database of 400,000 surnames and towns), the Family Tree of the Jewish People (with more than 3 million people listed), *ShtetLinks* (for over

200 communities), *Yizkor* book translations. In addition, there are sections on special interest groups, frequently asked questions (FAQs) and much more.

3.1.2 The Jewish Genealogical Society of Great Britain (JGSGB)

www.jgsgb.org.uk
The Society's website includes details of membership, the library catalogue, JGSGB Family Finder, special interest groups, programme of events and much more.

3.1.3 Jewish Communities and Records-UK (JCR-UK)

www.jewishgen.org/JCR-UK
The aim of JCR-UK is to record in electronic format genealogical and other community-related information about UK Jewish communities (England, Scotland, Wales, Northern Ireland and the Channel Islands) and make this information freely available via the Internet. Information is included about each individual Jewish community.

3.1.4 Susser Archive

www.jewishgen.org/JCR-UK/susser
The late Rabbi Dr Bernard Susser was born in 1930 in north-west London. The above archives include his records and transcriptions of communities in south-west England, such as those in Exeter, Falmouth, Penzance and Plymouth.

3.1.5 Moving Here

www.movinghere.org.uk
Moving Here is a database of over 200,000 digitized items related to migration to England over the last 200 years. It is led by The National Archives. There is a section of Jewish migration and immigration to the UK between the periods of 1885–1945 under the main heading of Migration Histories. There is also a list of suggested reading.

Jews' Free School (JFS) Admission Registers for both boys and girls are also on the above website and may be downloaded without charge. Enter LMA/4046 in the search field to find the list of files available.

3.1.6 Ancestry.co.uk

www.ancestry.co.uk

This is the UK's largest and most popular family history site, offering members access to 730 million searchable names. The site enables members to explore their family's history by viewing censuses for England, Wales and Scotland (1841–1901), England and Wales birth, marriage and death records (1837–2005), British Telecom (BT) phone books (1880–1984) and other records dating back before the 1300s. In addition, it has the world's largest collection of family trees, with more than 290 million names from over 100 countries in 3.2 million member trees.

3.1.7 Cyndi's List

www.cyndislist.com
www.cyndislist.com/jewish.htm

Cyndi's List has more than 200,000 links to websites, each with a genealogical connection. There is a categorized and cross-referenced index to genealogical resources on the Internet, and a list of links that point you to genealogical research sites online. Links are to most countries.

3.1.8 The Survey of Jewish Archives in the UK and Ireland

www.archives.soton.ac.uk/jewish

This database is part of the University of Southampton's Special Collections Database and contains descriptions of Jewish archive material held in archive repositories and private collections in the UK and Ireland, together with references to material of relevance to Anglo-Jewry held elsewhere. You can either search the entire database or any of the following sections:

• papers of Jewish individuals and families

• papers of Jewish organizations and congregations

• papers relating to communities and to Jewish-related subjects.

3.1.9 Family Search

www.familysearch.org

This website's FAQs cover a number of issues and are extremely helpful. The International Genealogical Index (IGI) index entries are also available online.

3.1.10 BBC Family History

www.bbc.co.uk/history/familyhistory
This website is designed to help you explore your family's past.

3.1.11 New York City Death Index

www.italiangen.org/NYCDEATH.STM
The index covers the years 1891–4 for Manhattan only, 1895–7 for Manhattan and Brooklyn only, and 1898–1948 for all boroughs.

3.1.12 Findmypast: (previously 1837 Online)

www.findmypast.com/HomeServlet
This website includes passenger lists leaving the UK, military records, births, marriages and deaths, military records, census records, migration, occupations and directories.

OUTWARD PASSENGER LISTS FROM THE UK
www.ancestorsonboard.com
This is a new database which features the BT27 outward passenger lists for long-distance voyages leaving the British Isles from 1960 right back to 1890. There are records of 30 million passengers on thousands of ships sailing to destinations worldwide. You can search for records of individuals or groups of people leaving for destinations including Australia, Canada, India, New Zealand, South Africa and USA featuring ports such as Boston, Philadelphia and New York. To view these exciting new records and original documents you will need to buy pay-per-view units from the *findmypast.com* website.

3.1.13 Free BMD

http://freebmd.rootsweb.com
FreeBMD is an ongoing project, the aim of which is to transcribe the General Register Office's (GRO) civil registration index of births, marriages and deaths for England and Wales, and to provide free Internet access to the transcribed records.

The recording of births, marriages and deaths was started in 1837 and is one of the most significant resources for genealogical research. The transcribing of the records is carried out by teams of dedicated volunteers and contains index information for the period 1837–1983. If you wish to view the up-to-date information on the coverage for each year go to *www.freebmd.org.uk/progress.shtml*.

3.1.14 GENUKI

www.genuki.org.uk – *www.genuki.org.uk/big*

GENUKI gives information and a list of sources for each geographical area or county. In addition, it lists many genealogical topics. There is also a section listing all the Register Offices in England and Wales (see *www.genuki.org. uk:8080/big/eng/RegOffice*).

3.1.15 The Historical Directories website

www.historicaldirectories.org

Historical Directories is a digital library of local and trade directories for England and Wales, from 1750 to 1919. It contains high quality reproductions of comparatively rare books, essential tools for research into local and genealogical history.

3.1.16 The 1901 Census for England and Wales

www.1901census.nationalarchives.gov.uk

Here you can search over 32 million people living in England and Wales in 1901 and view images of the original census documents. There is a charge for searches.

3.1.17 British Jewry website

www.british-jewry.org.uk

This is a forum for anyone researching British Jewry, whether your ancestors were just 'passing through' or were permanent members of British society. Posts relating to all aspects of life for British Jews as well as research methods, success stories and genealogy will be welcomed.

3.1.18 Jewish mailing lists – worldwide

www.rootsweb.com~jfuller/gen_mail_jewish.html

3.1.19 London Gazette

www.gazettes-online.co.uk

The London, Edinburgh, and Belfast gazettes are the official newspapers of record in the United Kingdom. Several legal notices, including insolvency notices, are required by law to be published in the gazettes. The *London Gazette* includes official notifications of naturalizations, bankruptcies and war medals.

The Stationery Office, on behalf of HMSO, have digitized much of the *London Gazette* archive. Access is free of charge. You can currently search the years from 1752 to 1998.

3.1.20 Proceedings of the Old Bailey – Jewish Communities of London

www.oldbaileyonline.org/history/communities/jewish.html

This section of the online database covers the Jewish communities of London. It explains how to search the database and gives the various keyword search terms that should produce a substantial number of examples relating to the Jewish community. There is also a bibliography and historical background. Jewish street traders have a significant presence in the Proceedings, frequently being accused of handling stolen goods. They also appear as victims of many crimes, and, in some trials, their accents and grammar are transcribed phonetically.

3.1.21 Search the archives/Documents Online

www.nationalarchives.gov.uk/searchthearchives

Here you can consult First World War medal rolls and wills of the Prerogative Court of Canterbury (PCC). This was the main court administering wills (1384–1858) and where most wills of Jews in this period were proved.

3.1.22 General Register Office (GRO)

www.gro.gov.uk/gro/content/certificate

Birth, marriage and death certificates for England and Wales may be ordered via this website.

3.1.23 PROCAT

www.nationalarchives.gov.uk/catalogue

The catalogue contains 10 million descriptions of documents from central government, courts of law and other UK national bodies, including records on family history, medieval tax, criminal trials, the history of many countries and many other subjects.

3.1.24 AIM 25

www.aim25.ac.uk/index.stm

If your ancestors were educated or employed in London over the course of the nineteenth and twentieth centuries you may find this website useful. AIM25 is a major project providing electronic access to collection-level descriptions of the archives of over ninety higher education institutions and learned societies within the greater London area. The website is updated regularly.

3.1.25 Sephardic Jewish genealogy

www.sephardim.com

If you are researching your Sephardic family history then this is where I would look first.

3.1.26 Sephardic genealogy resources

www.orthohelp.com/geneal/sefpage2.htm

Here you can find websites, articles, news lists and archives.

3.1.27 Jewish Virtual Library

The Jewish population of the world *http://tinyurl.com/29u2gw*. An extremely informative website.

3.1.28 Jewish Community of the South Manchester suburb of Didsbury, 1891–1914

www.jmaine.co.uk/jewishresearch.htm

This is a socio-economic comparison with the northern sector of the city's Jewry (initially for Open University Project Report Course DA301 1996), by Julia Maine. The paper explores the Jewish community of Didsbury, a middle-class suburb five miles south of the city of Manchester, during the period 1891–1914. There is a sample database of Didsbury's Jewish residents in 1905, with names and addresses. The website also has a discussion group.

3.1.29 Jgene wiki

www.jgene.org

Every day, more and more online genealogy resources are added to the Internet, which will be of great benefit to anyone researching their family tree.

This wiki (an online resource which allows users to add information) aims to bring together all Jewish genealogy links, resources and databases. All registered users can update and contribute to the site.

3.1.30 One-Step webpage

http://stevemorse.org
This covers the following records: Ellis Island; New York passenger/manifests/ship lists (1820–1957); ship pictures; ships and fleets; castle garden; Canadian, New York and British census; Holocaust; characters in foreign alphabets and much more.

3.1.31 Routes to Roots Foundation

www.rtrfoundation.org
The Routes to Roots Foundation was established in 1994 and involves the survey, study, research, inventory and documentation of Jewish material, archives and Judaica in Eastern European archives (Belarus, Lithuania, Moldova, Poland and the Ukraine).

3.1.32 The Rothschild Archives

www.rothschildarchive.org
The Rothschild Archive was established in 1978 to preserve and arrange the record of a family that is widely recognized for the major contribution it has made to the economic, political and social history of many countries throughout the world. The archive continues to reflect the many facets of the family's history and maintains an international research centre for the furtherance of study in these fields. The research centre is based in London, and the website has been developed to make the contents of the archive more readily available to remote users. The site aims to cater for the needs of all Rothschild Archive researchers.

3.1.33 Rabbinic Genealogy Special Interest Group (SIG)

www.jewishgen.org/Rabbinic
This is a forum for those interested in rabbinic genealogy or researching within any geographic area or time period.

3.1.34 United Kingdom National Inventory of War Memorials

www.ukniwm.org.uk

There are an estimated 70,000 war memorials throughout the UK in many differing forms, from the frequently-seen community crosses or plaques to buildings, lychgates, gardens, hospitals, organs, chapels and windows. The UK National Inventory of War Memorials database marks the unique place that they have in our nation's history and provides for the first time a UK-wide database of these memorials commemorating all conflicts, not just those of the First and Second World Wars.

3.1.35 Rootsweb-World Connect Project

www.rootsweb.com

The World Connect Project is a database of family trees submitted by thousands of RootsWeb.com researchers. There are currently more than 372,595,410 ancestor names. Go to RootsWeb's Guide to 'Tracing Family Trees' – 'Countries/Ethnic Groups' – then either 'Jewish' or 'Guide 25'.

3.1.36 Rootsweb – Surname List (RSL)

www.rootsweb.com

The RootsWeb Surname List (RSL) is a registry of more than 1,194,708 surname entries that have been submitted by more than 296,812 online genealogists. Associated with each surname are dates, locations and information about how to contact the person who submitted the surname.

3.1.37 Babelfish

http:babelfish.altavista.com/tr

This site translates speech from one language to another.

3.1.38 Jewish Web Index

http://jewishwebindex.com/index.htm

This website is owned by Ted Margulis. It includes information on the Holocaust, a Yiddish dictionary and a lot more.

3.1.39 Jewish genealogy links

www.pitt.edu/~meisel/jewish/about.htm

Jewish Genealogy Links (JGL) is maintained by Matthew Meisel and is a collection of links to sites helpful to those researching their Jewish roots. The website includes a surname dictionary, lists of archives, information on the Holocaust and Jewish orphanages.

3.1.40 USGen Web Project

www.usgenweb.org

This website is run by a group of volunteers working together to provide free genealogy websites for genealogical research in every county and every state of the United States. This project is non-commercial and fully committed to free genealogy access for everyone. This is an excellent website if you need to carry out research in the USA. It mentions some Jewish areas of interest.

Chapter 4

PUBLIC RECORDS

This chapter explains how to use information from public records to further your research. You may have heard of an ancestor but you have no proof that he or she existed. Public records may prove that they actually did exist, and you can then start to match up Jewish records. Conversely, you might find a Jewish record first and want more from the civil one.

It is very important to look at original documents or documents on microfilm, since transcriptions on the Internet often do not contain the correct detail or spelling.

4.1 What are public records?

These are records kept by governmental and other public bodies for all kinds of purposes; usually we think of our birth, marriage and death certificates (known as vital records), but there are also wills, electoral registers, census records, court records and military records. Records such as membership lists of professional bodies may not be public, but the names of committee members could be and might include an ancestor's name. If you know that your ancestor was a member of a professional body such as the Royal College of Surgeons of England, it may be worth writing to the archivist for further information. In addition anything published is a public record, so official newspapers such as the *London Gazette* fall into this category.

4.2 How do I start?

Unless you know there is an illustrious relative in the family with whom you claim relationship, you will work backwards. If you have talked to members of your family, you may have some ideas on where to begin, but let's suppose you have little or no information.

4.2.1 Start with yourself

If you know the names of your grandparents you could start your search further back. A full birth certificate gives date and place of birth, baby's forename(s) (if decided at time of registration), sex, father's name and occupation, mother's name and maiden name, and name, address and description of the informant. A 'short' certificate will show only the baby's forename(s) (if decided at time of registration), surname, sex and date of birth (*see 1.4*). Both these forms of certificate will have an entry number to link back to the original registration.

Be warned: if the parents were not married or if the mother was a single parent, the father may not be named.

4.3 Adoption

If you were adopted, and are over 18 years of age, you are allowed to see your original pre-adoption certificate. Unfortunately, *only* the adoptee is allowed to see the certificate, so if you discover that a parent or grandparent was adopted you may not be able to trace part of your genetic line. However, if you are interested in genealogy you may still find plenty of interest in another branch of your family.

If the parents are named on the birth certificate and appear to be married, the information can be used to trace their marriage certificate and thence their parents' names. The marriage certificate also contains details of the occupations of the groom and the fathers of the bride and groom if they were alive at the time of the marriage. *Adoption Search Reunion has a database to help people find out where adoption records are held (see www.adoptionsearchreunion.org.uk).*

4.4 Civil Registration

Civil Registration began in 1837 in England and Wales, 1855 in Scotland and 1864 in Ireland. However, registration was initially not compulsory in England and Wales. Whilst it was necessary to go through the registration process before a burial took place, there was no incentive to register births. It was the Registrar who had the incentive by being paid according to the number of registrations of births, marriages and deaths. Compulsion to register came through the Births and Deaths Registration Act 1874, which tightened up registration procedures in England and Wales.

Therefore, if you are looking at the period from 1837 to about 1870, the civil record for which you are looking may not exist. For Jewish persons, you might have to look for a Jewish burial record instead of a civil death registration. Synagogue burial records can provide useful clues for matching up families. For example, in one case four burials for a family where the surname was similar but not identical proved to be cousins. This was identified because all four children had the same grandfather according to their fathers' Hebrew names. Subsequently, further research proved this was correct.

The same also applies to marriage records. You may discover that families are related if you look at the Hebrew names of the bridegroom's father, especially if he has a common English name such as Davis.

Further reading
If you are unable to read Hebrew, the following will help you with reading Hebrew names, Jewish gravestones and other items of interest relating to family history: Rosemary Wenzerul, *Jewish Ancestors: A Guide to Reading Hebrew Inscriptions and Documents* (Jewish Genealogical Society of Great Britain, 2005: ISBN 0-9537669-6-9).

4.5 The National Archives (TNA)

Ruskin Avenue, Kew, Surrey, TW9 4DU
Tel: 020 8876 3444   Fax: 020 8392 5286
Website: *www.nationalarchives.gov.uk*
Since the Family Record Centre merged with the National Archives, everything is now under one roof. Kew is a treasure house when beginning genealogy; records include naturalizations and armed forces records. It is necessary to plan visits carefully in advance so that you are aware of all relevant dates and so on.

Research at TNA is fascinating, but can be very time-consuming. A reader's ticket is issued on the spot, on presentation of acceptable proof of identity documents. Telephone in advance if in doubt.

Amanda Bevan's *Tracing your Ancestors at the National Archives; the Website and Beyond* (ISBN: 1-903365-89-9) is the PRO 'Bible', and contains much useful information. For example, if you have an ancestor who was a coastguard, a member of the Royal Navy or any other armed force, a doctor or lawyer, this book will tell you where records may be found. Any medals awarded to personnel are all listed and the records of all servicemen in the First World War are in the process of being copied and made available.

4.5.1 Passport registers

Registers of names exist from 1795 to 1948. The registers give the number, date of issue and name. Before the 1920s the destination of the journey is also shown. This was because up until then the passport was a sheet of paper issued for a specific journey. From the early 1920s a book was issued and hence the registers do not contain a destination. Whilst entry was not restricted, migrants to the USA and the British colonies did not require passports. Indexes exist from 1851 to 1916 with a gap from 1863 to 1873. The registers and the indexes are in book form. From 1920 there is roughly one book per month. Details can be found in the PRO PROCAT catalogue under FO610.

4.5.2 Internments

Many Jews were interned as aliens during the two world wars. Some records are available at the National Archives at Kew (*see 4.5.4*).

4.5.3 Shipping records

These are in document classes BT26 (inwards, i.e. arriving passengers), BT27 (outwards, i.e. departing passengers). Class BT32 lists the ships that arrived and departed from each port. The passenger lists are arranged by British port from 1890, under name of ship, and only to and from places outside Europe. There are also extensive records from 1832 to 1869, which include some from Europe. Information given for arriving passengers can include name, age, occupation, proposed address in Britain and the date of entry, but often had just the surname. As these records are very bulky and lack an index, search time is lengthy and the resultant information is not always useful. Series BT27 is available online (*www.ancestorsonboard.com/static/about.html*) and is searchable by name.

4.5.4 Military records *(see also Chapter 11)*

The National Archives has records going back well into the seventeenth century, but most Jewish people will be interested in records after 1850 or so. TNA has microfilmed the records of all First World War personnel, and you can find out which First World War medals were awarded to any person. TNA website gives details of the records available: not all First World War records are in existence because some were destroyed in the Second World War. Those records that were damaged but not destroyed have been microfilmed and are only for privates and non-commissioned officers. In the eighteenth century Jews were involved with the Navy. Initially they acted as naval agents – when sailors in the Royal Navy captured an enemy ship all the crew shared in the prize. Because they were away for months at a time the agents acted by providing money up front and collecting the prize. When this practice ended many of the agents became military tailors in the naval ports (see Geoffrey Green, *The Royal Navy and Anglo Jewry 1740–1820*).

For the Second World War, TNA has lists of some aliens who were exempted from internment. Copies of the exemption certificates contain biographical details and the place of origin as well as their address (in the 1940s); there may also be some other records available.

It is well worth looking at the First World War British Jewry Book of Honour. In addition, the Commonwealth War Graves Commission has an excellent website, which gives burial details, cemetery location, name and address of next of kin and in most cases details of the battle for both world wars. All honours are also recorded in the *London Gazette*.

4.5.5 Naturalization records

Indexes under surnames (document class HO1) indicate surname, first name, naturalization date and place, country of origin, and cover the years 1844–1900, 1901–10, 1911–14, 1915–24, 1925–30, and 1931–5. Staff will explain how to order the original certificates and the 'background papers'. Certificates (document class HO334) give name, address, occupation, place and date of birth, nationality, marital status, first name of wife, names and nationality of parents (not usually mother's maiden name). Background papers (document class HO144) include the application. Early ones (to around 1900) give date and place of birth, parents, names and ages of children, residences in UK; middle ones (around 1920s) add wife's name, date and place of marriage, details of education and occupation, full police report; later ones (1930s) can add details of siblings and education or occupation before arrival. Availability seems to vary – from the late eighteenth century until 1940.

Individuals' naturalization papers may be seen. They contain the person's application, various supporting statements, a police report, and sometimes records of payments to a friendly society that helped with the naturalization. They also contain a copy of the person's oath of allegiance (which also appears in the *London Gazette* with their address and the date they took the oath). There are details of the applicant's family, place of origin, parents' names and length of residence. These records contain a wealth of detail and a slice of social history: many of the occupations mentioned have disappeared. The place of origin can be located by using something like the Encarta atlas. However, you will find that the information changes with the date; the later the date the more information. The background papers are also secret for seventy-five years, though one can some-times obtain access to them. When you find the naturalization date you can search the *London Gazette* archive free and find the naturalization listed. If you have some idea of your ancestor's date of naturalization and country of origin you can search for the date before trying to access the papers.

4.5.6 Vital records (England and Wales)

The public search room has indexes to births, marriages and deaths from 1837 to the present; arranged alphabetically by surname, by quarters (ending March, June, September, December) to 1983; from 1984, alphabetically by surname by year. It is necessary to quote the reference numbers in indexes when ordering copies of certificates, (there is a charge for certificates). These will be mailed within a few days.

The Office of National Statistics (ONS) intends to close its public search facility, currently located at the Family Records Centre (FRC) in Islington, and instead to make indexes available at The National Archives (TNA) in Kew. The relocation is expected to be complete by spring 2008. The services currently provided by ONS in Islington will then cease. For updates and news on the above situation, please go to the General Registry Office website (*www.gro.gov.uk/gro/content*). If you visit their website you can see the section on wills and probate records and the list of helpful information sheets they offer.

If you have a common name, you might need to get the certificates to confirm it is correct; if your name is sufficiently unusual you will not need to do this. Before you rush out to buy any certificates, look at the free BMD Indexes on Rootsweb (*http://freebmd.rootsweb.com*) to find the registration reference and then use it to order by post for a nominal fee.

Birth certificates give date, place, father, mother (including maiden name), father's occupation and the name and address of the informant. If the name of the father is left blank on the certificate, then the birth was illegitimate. If the exact time of birth is shown, then the child may have been a twin or triplet.

Marriage certificates give date and place of marriage, names and ages of couple, occupations, addresses, names and occupations of fathers and witnesses. In the early part of the nineteenth century, the age was often shown as 'of full age', that is, 21 or over.

Death certificates give date and place of death, name, age and occupation, cause of death, signature, description and residence of informant. With effect from 1 April 1969, the deceased's date and place of birth are also given on the death certificate. In addition, the maiden name of both married and widowed women are also shown.

Further reading
The excellent booklet 'A Quick Guide to Using the Indexes' is available free from The National Archives.

4.5.7 Marriage records

These can be searched by the wife or husband's name, though after 1911 marriages are cross-referenced to spouses (useful if one of your names is common). Having found the names that match, you can get the certificate. If you have two alternatives the records office can help you sort out which you want.

Do not be too surprised if you find no evidence of a marriage certificate and/or children born out of wedlock. Illegitimacy was more common than perhaps we realize. However, if a couple appeared to be living together these children were not necessarily registered as illegitimate because the registrars probably did not ask for evidence of marriage. You are likely to find evidence of pregnant brides where the child arrived immediately after the wedding. Single (unmarried) mothers also occur in some census records. Civil death records can be searched in the same way. They may not be as accurate as any other record as the information depended on the informant, who may have had to guess at someone's age, for example. After 1969 the deaths indexes usually show date and place of birth. However, sometimes you can use the death record to help you search for a burial record.

4.5.8 Census records

Census records exist for the years 1841, 1851, 1861, 1871, 1881, 1891 and 1901. The census was taken every ten years from 1801, except in 1941. The census years of relevance to genealogists are 1841–1901. This is because the earlier censuses lack individual names and the later ones are secret for 100 years. All the censuses from 1841 were taken as of midnight on a Sunday and are available to researchers.

Year	Census Dates	Class
1801	Tues 10 March	
1811	Mon 27 May	
1821	Mon 28 May	
1831	Mon 30 May	
1841	Sun 6 June	HO107
1851	Sun 30 March	HO107
1861	Sun 7 April	RG09
1871	Sun 2 April	RG10
1881	Sun 3 April	RG11
1891	Sun 5April	RG12
1901	Sun 31 March	RG13
1911	Sun 2 April	Not yet released
1921	Sun 19 June	Not yet released
1931	Sun 26 April	Destroyed by fire in WWII
1941	No census	Due to WWII
1951	Sun 8 April	Not yet released
1961	Sun 23 April	Not yet released
1971	Sun 25 April	Not yet released
1981	Sun 5 April	Not yet released
1991	Sun 21 April	Not yet released
2001	Sun 29 April	Not yet released

Census dates 1801–2001.

To search on microfilm or fiche, you need the relevant address because there is no index to names. The census lists all residents by name, age, relationship to the head of household and place of birth (district in UK, otherwise country). See below for online searches.

The 1851 census for Whitechapel has been indexed by surname and is available at the Family Records Centre.

The TNA publication *Making Sense of the Census* gives useful information about using the census but emphasizes that an address is required to be able to search in the indexes. Where you are using a database or Internet facility this is not always necessary. In some places the records were not preserved: if that is the case you are advised to search an earlier or later census. Lists of areas where the census is missing are given in *Making Sense of the Census* and on websites which supply census data.

The 1881 census is available on CD-ROM at some Libraries such as the Church of the Latter Day Saints. This can be useful if you do not have your own

1881 British Census

Dwelling: **1 Sandys Row**
Census Place: **St Botolph Bishopsgate, London, Middlesex, England**
Source: **FHL Film 1341080**   **PRO Ref RG11**   **Piece 0371**   **Folio 53**   **Page 24**

	Marr	Age	Sex	Birthplace
Abraham GOLDSTEIN	**M**	**49**	**M**	**Poland**
Rel: **Head**				
Occ: **Teacher Of Hebrew**				
Amelia GOLDSTEIN	**M**	**46**	**F**	**Bishopsgate, Middlesex, England**
Rel: **Wife**				
Levy GOLDSTEIN	**U**	**20**	**M**	**Norwich, Norfolk, England**
Rel: **Son**				
Occ: **Jeweller**				
Joseph GOLDSTEIN	**U**	**18**	**M**	**Gt Yarmouth, Norfolk, England**
Rel: **Son**				
Occ: **Boot Whouseman**				
Nehimiah GOLDSTEIN	**U**	**16**	**M**	**Gt Yarmouth, Norfolk, England**
Rel: **Son**				
Occ: **Teacher Of Hebrew**				
Maria GOLDSTEIN		**14**	**F**	**Gt Yarmouth, Norfolk, England**
Rel: **Daugh**				
Occ: **Seamstress**				
Esther GOLDSTEIN		**12**	**F**	**Shoreditch, Middlesex, England**
Rel: **Daugh**				
Occ: **Scholar**				
Simon GOLDSTEIN		**9**	**M**	**Shoreditch, Middlesex, England**
Rel: **Son**				
Occ: **Scholar**				
Isaac GOLDSTEIN		**7**	**M**	**Bishopsgate, Middlesex, England**
Rel: **Son**				
Occ: **Scholar**				
Francis GOLDSTEIN		**6**	**F**	**Bishopsgate, Middlesex, England**
Rel: **Daugh**				
Occ: **Scholar**				
Henry GOLDSTEIN		**4**	**M**	**Bishopsgate, Middlesex, England**
Rel: **Son**				

Surname incorrect - should be
GOLDSTON

Extract from the 1891 census, showing incorrect spelling of a surname.

computer or access to the Internet. Some local libraries also have the relevant CD for their area and you should contact the library direct to check availability.

The 1881 census has been indexed by surname and is available at *www. familysearch.org*. This site is very useful and also includes census records for the United States.

On the 1891 census, if you look very carefully you will see an over-marking which has been put in by the enumerator or someone else, for example, 'job', 'gold' (a jeweller) '*independent means*' – a person who has sufficient assets to provide an income without having to work. Once you can find someone who was alive in one of these census years you can start to use the census to lead you further backwards and outwards. A useful guide when you have your census returns is *Making Sense of the Census*, which gives information about the forms and the questions asked for all the censuses from 1841 to 1901.

The 1901 census asked for birthplace, nationality, activity, whether employed, or apprentice, employment status, occupation and workplace (restricted to those carrying on a trade or working at home). People were also asked about infirmity – deafness, dumbness, blindness and lameness (foreshadowing today's questions about disability).This appears on the right-hand column of the form in 1901.

Since the enumerator could not challenge any information given, in some cases the details are incorrect. For example, you may find that one of your own ancestors, who you know was born in New York, put himself down in the census as being British-born.

When searching, try as many variants of a surname as possible if you do not immediately find what you are searching for. Although searching the census might look daunting, remember that the population of Great Britain was considerably smaller in the nineteenth century, only 38 million in 1901 and 20 million in 1851.

If you are looking at a copy of a census record, a single address may consist of several households but lines across one of the columns show the demarcation between each household. All persons living at an address should have been included, together with their age, place of birth, occupation and relationship to the head of the household. The age given may not always be accurate; often people gave their wrong age or used poetic licence! In 1841 the age was given plus or minus five years. Once you have found your ancestor on a census, it is well worth looking at the same address for ten years earlier: you may find they stayed there. Alternatively, you may find they were in the same neighbourhood or even in the same street. Once you have the names and ages of all the siblings of a particular generation, you can start to search for their births and so on, for each person on the list, provided they were in Great Britain. These can lead you to previous addresses of the family. You may also find that people's names change. For example, in 1871 a lady was called Vogellina; in 1881 she was Foglena and by 1891 she called herself Sophia!

If you find a person described as 'son-in-law' and they are unmarried it will probably mean a stepchild where they are living with one parent and a step-parent. It is also not unusual to find second or third marriages, as widows and widowers often remarried. You may also find couples who appear to be married but no record of marriage can be found: see the note above on marriage records.

You may also find that children are missing in subsequent census records. If this is the case they could have died, bearing in mind that infant and child mortality rates were higher in the nineteenth century than today. If you discover that one of your ancestors appears on a record of an institution, look at the first page of the record to find out the name and location of the institution. You may be able to find out if there are any records of that institution available. For example, Norwood Orphanage (formerly the Jews' Orphan Asylum), a famous Jewish orphanage, had children who lived there for a few years and then returned to their families. Children might enter when their father died suddenly at an early age and two years later return to their mother when family circumstances had improved. Other institutions may include hospitals and workhouses.

For most censuses a map, such as a reprint from Ordnance Survey maps, may be useful if you are not searching online. You may have to search whole neighbourhoods, since each census used different enumeration districts (sections of a parish allocated to a census enumerator for collecting data). Look up the enumeration districts for the streets you are interested in and then go through the records.

4.5.9 Censuses 1841 to 1901

These are all available online, though a subscription may be required for access. However, searching microfiches is more reliable because transcriptions often do not record the correct information. In some cases you may find that the surname is omitted. At The National Archives, online searches are free, although you may have to pay for copies. *Ancestry.com* and *findmypast.com* are two of a number of sites where you pay for a subscription and have access to various records in addition to the census.

4.5.10 Census 1911

The 1911 census is going to become available early, at least in part. The National Archives has announced two services in advance of the official 2012 full release date.

In January 2007, TNA offered a limited research service where the address of an individual in the 1911 census was already known. There is a non-refundable search charge of £45. Meanwhile, TNA have said it hopes to offer a searchable online service in early 2009, with key sensitive information withheld until January 2012. The Chief Executive has said that TNA will digitize the 1911 census as quickly as possible (for regular updates, see *www.nationalarchives.gov.uk/1911census*).

4.5.11 How to calculate ages from census returns

Providing your ancestor gave their correct age on the census form, you can work out roughly when they were born. For example, if your relative was shown as aged 25 in the 1851 census, deduct the age from the year (census year 1851 minus age 25 = 1826, therefore, they would have been born between 30 March 1826, when the census was taken, and 31 March the previous year, 1825).

4.6 Wills and administration

Principal Registry of the Family Division, 1st Avenue House, 42-49 High Holborn, London, W1V 6NP
Tel: 020 7947 6000 Fax: 020 7947 7027
Probate Registry (same address) Tel: 020 7947 6939
(Records were previously held at Somerset House)

For England and Wales these records date from 1858. They are arranged annually in alphabetical order by surname.

4.6.1 Wills

Wills for England and Wales after 1858 are obtainable from the Principal Registry of the Family Division. For earlier wills The National Archives (previously held at the Family Record Centre) has microfilm copies of the Principal Prerogative Court of Canterbury (PCC) for 1384–1858. This was the High Court for the southern half of the country. It has indexes of wills from 1858–1943. Wills can be searched online (*www.familyrecords.gov.uk/frc/research/willsmain.htm*). However, if you don't find a will online, you may have to look at the microfiches since not all wills appear to have been recorded online. The northern counterpart was the Principal Prerogative Court of York (PCY).

Wills are useful in clarifying relationships. For example, they may mention sons-in-law or daughters-in-law or other in-laws you may not know about. If someone remarried there may be a will containing names you are unaware of, especially if the person had a new family. They can also contain details of possessions. You may read about an object or document that you know of or even possess, such as 'my best china tea set she always admired', in an extract from a will.

Probate copies of wills may also be found at the London Metropolitan Archives (LMA). For full details of the LMA holdings, see their information leaflet No. 6, 'Wills in London Metropolitan Archives and Elsewhere'. If you discover that your ancestor left a will it is worth looking at the *Jewish Chronicle* archive or *The Times* (subscriptions required for online viewing) archives, as they often published details of wills, and still do today. For example, in a report of one will, the names of all the person's children and some of their addresses could be found, as each were named. The *London Gazette* (and also its sister gazettes) carries announcements about wills – if a person was intestate, adverts often ask for any interested persons to contact solicitors.

4.7 Electoral registers

These are based on address and may be seen in main public libraries in each borough, but they are not always complete. London registers are also available at the London Metropolitan Archives. Universal suffrage has only been around since 1928, but some women over 30 could vote in 1918. Your local archive or history library might have copies of old electoral registers. In the early part of the century you could only vote if you were a ratepayer. A complete present day set for the UK is stored at The National Archives. Under addresses, there are lists of those eligible to vote: 1884–1918, men only; from 1918, women over 30 if householders or wives of householders, and all men over 21; from 1928, all over 21; from 1940s, all over 18.

4.8 Trade directories

If your ancestor had a trade or profession you may find their name in trade directories (e.g. Kelly's or Pigot's). Do not look in a trade directory for just one year, as you may well find an ancestor was listed only for the years when they paid, so there may be gaps.

Trade directories are the pre-telephone equivalent of the Yellow Pages phone directory combined with some aspects of post office directories. They contain the names of the gentry, clergy, professional people, merchants, and tradesmen who have their own businesses. In coastal counties they also list ships' captains and owners. In mining counties they list the mine company, the owner and the management employees. You will not usually find a tradesman if he was employed by someone else. These directories were used by travelling salesmen as a source of information as they made their rounds. Because of the use they were put to, they are organized by county, town and adjacent area, class and/or trade and occupation. They also give a potted history of each town or area.

Historical Directories is produced and owned by the University of Leicester. It is a digital library of local and trade directories for England and Wales from

1750-1919. This website (*www.historicaldirectories.org*) also includes the post office directories from 1840.

4.9 Telephone directories

British Telecom (BT) telephone directories are searchable online from 1880 to 1984 on *www.Ancestry.co.uk*. This is a very useful site because the directories were published annually, so changes of address can be followed.

Other useful websites are *www.192.com*, which has 600 million people and business records, and *www.infobel.com*, which will help you find anyone anywhere in the UK and in many foreign countries. This website includes comprehensive updated white and yellow pages for the whole United Kingdom. It is a free service that allows nationwide search throughout the country in English, French, Spanish, Dutch, German and Italian. (*See also 5.10 and 5.11.*)

Chapter 5

ARCHIVES

I will begin this chapter with the holdings of the London Metropolitan Archives (LMA) that are relevant to Jewish research. The LMA is the largest archive in the United Kingdom after The National Archives (TNA) and is one of the largest civic archives in the world.

5.1 London Metropolitan Archives (LMA)

40 Northampton Road, London, EC1R OHB
Tel: 020 7332 3820   Fax: 020 7833 9136
E-mail: ask.lma@cityoflondon.gov.uk
Website: *www.cityoflondon.gov.uk/Corporation*

The LMA is the largest local authority record office in the UK, with 55 kilometres of records dating back nearly 900 years. The archive has records from former county councils of London, Middlesex and Greater London. Main sources for family history include registers from over 800 parishes, poor law records and registers of electors, as well as maps, plans and photographs.

To download the 'Records of the Anglo-Jewish Community' from the LMA website, search on 'Records of the Anglo-Jewish Community' and a list will come up.

The LMA is a major repository for records of Anglo-Jewish organizations from 1591, such as the Chief Rabbi's Office, the Board of Deputies of British Jews, the Federation of Synagogues and the Jews' Temporary Shelter. A full list of records held by the LMA is shown later in this chapter.

5.1.1 Synagogue minute books and members' lists
Some of these are held at the LMA, but a letter of permission is needed from synagogue authorities to view them.

5.1.2 ELECTORAL REGISTERS

The LMA has a major collection of electoral registers for Middlesex (1832–1963), the County of London (1890–1939 and 1945–63), and the Greater London area (from 1964).

5.1.3 SCHOOL RECORDS

Microfilm of the admission and discharge registers of the many state schools in the Greater London area are held by the LMA. The archive also has some Jews' Free School records, which are not restricted. Of particular interest are the school's admission and discharge registers (1869–1939) for pupils (*see section on Computers in Genealogy under 'Moving Here' for free download*). These books are a wonderful source of information and the archives have good sets for schools such as Stepney Jewish and many other schools with large numbers of Jewish pupils. The LMA also holds the records of the former Westminster Jews' Free School.

5.1.4 HOSPITAL RECORDS

The LMA holds the London section of a national database of hospital records. This database is compiled by the TNA and the Contemporary Medical Archives Centre at the Wellcome Institute for the History of Medicine (183 Euston Road, London, NW1 2BE), and can be consulted at either institution. It covers hospital records and their repositories in England, Scotland and Wales. Generally the records include administrative and patient records which are subject to a closure period of 100 years by order of the Lord Chancellor. They also hold the archives of three major London teaching hospitals, Guy's, St Thomas's and Westminster Hospitals, as well as archives of many smaller local hospitals.

5.1.5 POOR JEWS' TEMPORARY SHELTER

The Poor Jews' Temporary Shelter at 82 Leman Street, London, E1 was a temporary home for many East European Jews en route to Australia, Canada, South Africa, South America and the USA. In 1906 it moved to 84 Leman Street. Every ship with Jewish migrants on board would be met by a representative from the shelter. It only accepted adult men. Women and children were cared for by the Jewish Association for the Protection of Girls, Women and Children.

A database containing the registers of shelter residents (over 43,000 Jews) during the period 1895–1914 has been constructed by the Department of History at the University of Leicester under the leadership of Professor Aubrey Newman and Dr John Graham Smith. The database can be searched on the website of the Kaplan Centre for Jewish Studies and Research at the University of Cape Town (*http://chrysalis.its.uct.ac.za/shelter/shelter.htm*).

5.1.6 SOUP KITCHEN FOR THE JEWISH POOR

Records are held at the LMA. Access is open. The soup kitchen for the Jewish poor was founded in 1854. It supplied soup, bread and meat twice weekly during the winter to the poor of the Jewish community. Originally in Fashion Street, Spitalfields, it transferred to 17–19 Butler Street, Spitalfields in 1902. The street name was changed to Brune Street in 1937. The kitchen ceased to function during the Second World War because of food rationing, and did not reopen afterwards.

Soup kitchen for the Jewish poor. (© Derek Wenzerul)

5.1.7 LIBRARY AND READING ROOM

The LMA has an extensive library with over 100,000 items. However, only around 10 per cent of these books are actually on the shelves. In addition, the LMA's Library holds source material on the Federation Synagogues, among which are the collection books of the Lodz Synagogue, Poland, c.1898, with members' names and addresses.

Records of the Anglo-Jewish community.

ACC/2712
United Synagogue and Predecessors – *Chief Executive, United Synagogue, 735 High Road, North Finchley, London, NW12 OUS.*

ACC/2793
World Jewish Relief (Central British Fund for World Jewish Relief) – *The Forum, 74/80 Camden Street, London, NW1 OEG.*

ACC/2805
Office of the Chief Rabbi – *Chief Executive, United Synagogue, 735 High Road, North Finchley, London, NW12 OUS.*

ACC/2886
West London Synagogue – *Executive Director, West London Synagogue, 35 Seymour Place, London, W1H 6AT.*

ACC/2893
The Federation of Synagogues – *Head of Administration, Federation of Synagogues, 65 Watford Way, Hendon, London, NW4 3AQ.*

ACC/2911
Western Synagogue – *President, Western Synagogue, Western Marble Arch Synagogue, 32 Great Cumberland Place, London, W1H 7DJ.*

ACC/2942
Food for the Jewish Poor – *The London Museum of Jewish Life, Sternberg Centre, 80 East End Road, Finchley, London, N3 2SY.*

ACC/2943
New Road Synagogue – *The London Museum of Jewish Life, Sternberg Centre, 80 East End Road, Finchley, London, N3 2SY.*

ACC/2944
Jewish Bread, Meat and Coal Society – *The London Museum of Jewish Life, Sternberg Centre, 80 East End Road, Finchley, London, N3 2SY.*

ACC/2980
The Kashrus Commission – *Chief Executive, United Synagogue, 735 High Road, North Finchley, London, NW12 OUS.*

ACC/2999
Jewish Memorial Council – *General Manager, Jewish Memorial Council, 25 Enford Street, London, W1H 2DD.*

ACC/3037
National Council for Jews in the Former Soviet Union – *Executive Director, Board of Deputies of British Jews, 5th Floor, Commonwealth House, 1-19 New Oxford Street, London, WC1A INF.*

ACC/3090
Jewish Health Organisation of Great Britain – *Executive Director, CBF World Jewish Relief, Drayton House, 30 Gordon Street, London, WC1H OAN.*

ACC/3121
Board of Deputies of British Jews – *Executive Director, Board of Deputies of British Jews, 5th Floor, Commonwealth House, 1-19 New Oxford Street, London, WC1A INF. Tel: 020 7543 5400*

ACC/3400
The London Beth Din – *Chief Executive, United Synagogue, 735 High Road, North Finchley, London, NW12 OUS. Tel: 020 8343 8989*

LMA/4180
London School of Jewish Studies (formerly Jews' College) – *Un-catalogued: available at 72 hours' notice.*

LMA/4184
Jews' Temporary Shelter – *Mr B Koschland, 23 Vincent Court, Bell Lane, London, NW4 2AN.*

H12/CH
Friern Hospital – *(Jewish patient records – closed to public access until they are over 100 years old).*

DL/C
Consistory Court of the Bishop of London – *contains material on some Jews both in connection with probate and marital litigation (the religious 'get' was a separate communal matter dealt with by the Beth Din).*

THE FOLLOWING DO NOT REQUIRE PERMISSION

ACC/2996
Victoria Club

ACC/3529
Liberal Jewish Synagogue

ACC/3686
London Society of Jews and Christians

LMA/4046
Jews' Free School (JFS)

LMA/4047 and LCC/EO
Westminster Jews' Free School, London School of Jewish Studies
(un-catalogued; available only at 72 hours' notice)

LMA/4071
Westminster Synagogue

LMA/4175
Women's International Zionist Organisation (WIZO)

5.2 Access to the Archives (A2A)

A2A, The National Archives, Kew, Richmond, Surrey, TW9 4DU
Tel: 020 8876 3444   Fax: 020 8487 9211
E-mail: a2a@nationalarchives.gov.uk
Website: *www.a2a.org.uk*

A2A allows you to search and browse for information about archives in England and Wales, dating from the eighth century to the present day. These archives are cared for in local record offices and libraries, universities, museums and national and specialist institutions across England and Wales, where they are made available to the public. The A2A database is a catalogue of more than 7.8 million files or documents located in 390 record offices. Many of the items are searchable by an individual's name.

If you are investigating your family history or carrying out a one-name study and would like to know more about your house, your street or your community in earlier years or if you have an interest in England's heritage and past, you will find the A2A database well worth a look.

5.3 Hackney Archives

43 De Beauvoir Road, London, N1 5SQ
Tel: 020 7241 2886   Fax: 020 7241 6688
E-mail: archives@hackney.gov.uk
Website: *www.hackney.gov.uk/index/hackney/archives.htm*

It is essential to make an appointment before visiting. The Hackney Archives department looks after the archives of Hackney, the administrative records of the borough council and its predecessors back to 1700, and of organizations and individuals within the borough. Services include a record search service for family historians who, for example, can order a search of the 1871 census or 1955 electoral registers – there is a charge for this service.

The Jewish community in Hackney dates back to 1674. By 1800 there was a considerable Jewish population, especially in Stamford Hill, where the Montefiore and Rothschilds families lived. Immigration brought certain favoured trades such as footwear, clothing and especially furniture-making. The archive has some interesting books such as M. Bernstein's *Stamford Hill and the Jews before 1915*. There is also a large collection of local directories (going well back into the nineteenth century), as well as useful electoral registers and census indexes.

5.4 Islington Local History Centre

Finsbury Library, 245 St. John Street, London, EC1V 4NB
Tel: 020 7527 7988 (appointments and enquiries)
E-mail: local.history@islington.gov.uk
Website: *www.islington.gov.uk/libraries*

As this is only a couple of minutes' walk from the LMA it is worth knowing about for those with any connections in Islington. There was a notable Jewish area near Canonbury Station, which sits between Highbury, Newington Green and Canonbury. Voters' lists pre-1900 are rather disappointing, but they have some early rating lists.

Family history sources include census returns for Islington and Finsbury (1841–1901), electoral registers (from 1870s onwards), parish registers for St Mary Islington, rate books, maps, photographs and a range of archive and published material. It is advisable to book an appointment to visit.

5.5 Norwood-Ravenswood Archives

Broadway House, 80–82 The Broadway, Stanmore, Middlesex, HA7 4HB
Tel: 020 8954 4555   Fax: 020 8420 6800
E-mail: norwood@norwood.org.uk
Website: *www.norwood.org.uk*
Archives: E-mail: betty.marks@norwood.org.uk
Tel: 0208 420 6848

This archive holds records for the Jews' Hospital and Orphanage Norwood. In 1795 the Jews' Hospital and Asylum in Mile End was established with ten boys and eight girls. In 1860 there were a hundred boys and forty girls. In 1928 the institution changed its name to the Jewish Orphanage and later to Norwood Orphanage. It closed in 1963. In 1996 Norwood merged with Ravenswood. Currently the archives of the merged organizations are being gathered together. There is a charge of around £25 for a search through the archives.

5.6 London School of Economics Archives and Rare Books Library

London School of Economics and Political Science, 10 Portugal Street, London, WC2A 2HD
Tel: 020 7955 7223   Fax: 020 7955 7454
Email: Document@lse.ac.uk
Website: *http://library-2.lse.ac.uk/archives/pdf/Jewish_notebooks. html*

Four notebooks from the Charles Booth collection relating to the Jewish community in London in the 1880s and 1890s have been digitized. One notebook contains various documents regarding Jews, including letters, booklets, interview notes and a list of synagogues. The notebook is from a series relating to religious influences in London in the late nineteenth century. The other three notebooks relate to textile trades, which in late nineteenth-century London included a high number of Jewish employers and workers. The volumes are from a series of notebooks consisting of data regarding trades and industries gathered from questionnaires and interviews of workers, trade union leaders and employers.

5.7 Tower Hamlets Local History Archives

Tower Hamlets Local History Archives, Bancroft Library,
277 Bancroft Road, London, E1 4DQ
Tel: 020 7364 1290 (Archives)   Fax: 020 7364 1292
E-mail: localhistory@towerhamlets.gov.uk
Website: *www.towerhamlets.gov.uk*

Tower Hamlets local history library and archive covering the area of the present-day London Borough of Tower Hamlets, the original East End of London which, until 1965, comprised the Boroughs of Bethnal Green, Poplar and Stepney.

If you are interested in a building in the borough, tracing your ancestors who lived here, doing a school or college project on some aspect of the borough or are just feeling nostalgic, this library may well be able to help you. It holds details of Princelet Street Synagogue marriages, including the original marriage authorization certificates. In addition, marriage notice books for Stepney from 1926 and Bethnal Green (1837–78 and 1920–65) contain marriage applications giving the date, names of couple, marital status, profession, age, address, length of residence in UK and place of intended marriage. The library has a wealth of material on the East End of London's local newspapers from 1857, and copies of the census and electoral registers may also be seen here.

5.8 City of Westminster Archives

10 St Ann's Street, London, SW1P 2DE
Tel: 020 7641 5180   Fax: 020 7641 5179
E-mail: archives@westminster.gov.uk
Website: *www.westminster.gov.uk/archives*

The centre's collections extend to over 5 kilometres of shelving. There are around 60,000 illustrations dating from Tudor times to the present day, and the earliest original item dates from 1256.

5.9 Records Office (City of London Records Office)

The Corporation of London Records Office
PO Box 270, Guildhall, London, EC2P 2EJ
Tel: 020 7332 1251   Fax: 020 7710 8682
E-mail: clro@corpoflondon.gov.uk
Website: *www.cityoflondon.gov.uk*

Note: the records held at the CLRO are now in the process of being relocated to the London Metropolitan Archives.

The CLRO holds the official archives of the Corporation of London, the local authority for the City of London square mile. Major classes of records in the CLRO include charters (1067–1957), administrative records (1275 to date), financial records, freedom records (1681–1940), architectural plans and drawings and much more.

If you had family members that were council members, sheriffs or aldermen of the City of London, the City of London Records Office has records of these going back to the Middle Ages.

5.10 British Telecom Archives (BT)

BT Group Archives, Third Floor, Holborn Telephone Exchange, 268–270 High Holborn, London, WC1V 7EE
Tel: 020 7440 4220   Fax: 020 7242 1967
E-mail: archives@bt.com
Website: *www.bt.com/archives*

These archives contain historical telephone directories, near complete sets of telephone directories for the whole country produced not only by BT but also by its predecessors including Post Office Telecommunications, the National Telephone Company and other private companies. Dating back to 1880, the year after the public telephone service was introduced into Great Britain, they are of particular interest to family and social historians.

5.11 Royal Mail Archives

Postal Heritage Trust, Freeling House, Phoenix Place, London, WC1X 0DL
Tel: 020 7239 2570   Fax: 020 7239 2576
E-mail: heritage@royalmail.com
Website: *www.royalmail.com/heritage*

The Royal Mail Archive contains records for the history of the post office over four centuries. For family history research the main sources are the appointment books (1734–74, 1831–1956) and establishment books (1742–1946). There are also records of pensions, postmasters/postmistresses, packet boat agents and captains as well as many other supporting sources.

5.12 Camden Local Studies and Archives Centre

Holborn Library, 32-38 Theobalds Road, London, WC1X 8PA
Tel: 020 7974 6342   Fax: 020 7974 6284
E-mail: localstudies@camden.gov.uk
Website: *www.camden.gov.uk/localstudies*

The Camden Local Studies and Archives Centre contains archives, printed material, illustrations and maps about the history of the area from the seventeenth century until the present day. Sources for family history research include rate books, electoral registers, local directories, local newspapers, monumental inscriptions and Highgate Cemetery registers. There may be some useful information relating to Jewish families in the area.

5.13 South Humberside Area Archive Office

Town Hall, Town Hall Square, Grimsby, DN31 1HX
Tel: 01472 323585   Fax: 01472 323582

This archive holds the records of the Grimsby Hebrew Congregation: B'nai B'rith registers of attendance (1954–67); Grimsby Hebrew Congregation: records related to Jewish Women's Guild and photocopies of personal papers (1876–1986); Grimsby Tent of the Lovers of Zion Chovevi Zion: copy articles of association and papers (1891–92: 1,032); Gerlis papers: material collected for published history of Jewish community of Grimsby (1986: 1,032); Grimsby Hebrew Congregation: copy of first minute book (1889–96). Grimsby Zionist Society: minutes (1948–85).

5.14 Hull City Archives

79 Lowgate, Kingston Upon Hull, HU1 1HN
Tel: 01482 615102   Fax: 01482 613051
E-mail: city.archives@hullcc.gov.uk
Website: *www.hullcc.gov.uk/archives/index.php*

Hull has a remarkable collection of sixteenth- and seventeenth-century borough records. These cast light on aspects of national and regional history as well as the history of the city itself. Some of these records have been transcribed and can be found at *www.hull.ac.uk/sp12*.

Hull was one of the ports of entry into this country for thousands of Jewish migrants from Eastern Europe, many of whom travelled on to the USA, Canada and South Africa. Many of the archive records held are described on A2A, the Access to Archives database. This contains catalogues describing archives held locally in England and Wales and dating from the eighth century to the present day. To search A2A visit their website (*www.a2a.org.uk/*; see also *www.movinghere.org.uk*). A full list of websites can be found on 'Gareth's List' on the family history section of Hull City Council's website (*www.hullcc.gov.uk/genealogy*).

5.15 Scottish Jewish Archives Centre

Garnethill Synagogue, 129 Hill Street, Glasgow, G3 6UB
Tel/Fax: 0141 332 4911
E-mail: info@sjac.org.uk
Website: *www.sjac.org.uk*

The Garnethill Synagogue was built in 1879. It was Glasgow's first purpose-built synagogue and the only one for Glasgow's Jewish population of 700. The

Garnethill Synagogue. (© Scottish Jewish Archives Centre)

archive centre, opened in 1987, is a national heritage information and research centre which collects documents, photographs and artefacts. It also houses an exhibition showing the history of the Jews in Scotland since the seventeenth century.

5.15.1 Jewish genealogy in Scotland

The first Jewish communities were established in Edinburgh in 1816 and in Glasgow in 1823. Small communities were founded later in the nineteenth century in Aberdeen and Dundee, but although their synagogues remain, the congregations are very small. At one time, there were also communities in Ayr, Dunfermline, Falkirk, Greenock and Inverness – all now defunct.

Civil records of births, marriages and deaths in Scotland since 1855, as well as census records, may be found in New Register House in Edinburgh. There is a daily search fee (currently £17), allowing access to all documents either on microfiche, or in many cases as scanned images on computer terminals. The Strathclyde Area Genealogy Centre in Glasgow offers access to the computer indexes, but holds film or fiche of the records only for the west of Scotland. The website *www.scotlandspeople.gov.uk* offers a fully searchable index of Scottish birth records (1855–1906); marriage records (1855–1931); death records (1855–1956), and censuses (1891–1901). Copies can be ordered by credit card.

Records of Jewish communities and individuals are held by the Scottish Jewish Archives Centre. These include minutes, membership lists, annual reports and yearbooks of synagogues and other communal organizations, synagogue registers, circumcision and burial lists, photographs, newspapers and press cuttings, oral history and videos, and personal papers. The centre also holds the computerized Historical Database of Scottish Jewry, which now contains 29,000 records.

Chapter 6

LIBRARIES AND MUSEUMS

It is important that attention be drawn to the fact that there is a wealth of information on family history in your local public library. If a specific book on Jewish family history is not available, it can always be ordered. Most libraries have sections for family history as well as some for reference only. In addition, many have computers with access to the Internet. If you do not have your own computer then this is an ideal way to find out more information (*see Chapter 3, which will give you some useful links to Jewish genealogical websites*).

Libraries

6.1 Bishopsgate Library

The Bishopsgate Institute and Foundation, 230 Bishopsgate, London, EC2M 4QH
Tel: 020 7392 9270   Fax: 020 7392 9275
Website: *www.bishopsgate.org.uk*

Bishopsgate Library provides a focal point for research into the history and topography of London, in particular the East End. It has unique and fascinating historical collections and continues to collect a broad range of books, pamphlets and archival material. In addition, the library holds research materials for local and family historians, and maintains general reference materials and current national and local newspapers.

6.2 British Library

96 Euston Road, London, NW1 2DB
Tel: 020 7412 7332 (visitor information)
E-mail: Visitor-Services@bl.uk
Website: *www.bl.uk*

The British Library holds 70,000 Hebrew printed books, 3,000 Hebrew manuscripts. The principal resources used for family history are in the India Office Records, for ancestors in British India, and in the newspapers at the Newspaper Library in Colindale (*see 6.3*). The library's extensive collections include electoral registers, directories, oral history, pedigrees, maps and patents. Please check their website for catalogues and opening hours of the different reading rooms.

6.3 British Library Newspaper Library

Colindale Avenue, London, NW9 5HE
Tel: 020 7412 7353 (Reading room)   Fax: 020 7412 7379
Email: newspaper@bl.uk
Website: *www.bl.uk/collections/newspapers.html*
(18 years or over, identification necessary, last admittance 4 p.m.)

Jewish Chronicle, *Jewish World* and many other Jewish newspapers from both the UK and abroad are available in the library. The *Voice of Jacob*, the *Jewish Standard*, the *Jewish World*, the *Hebrew Observer*, the *Jewish Record* and Yiddish papers. In addition, the following provincial newspapers are available, *The Jewish Echo*, *Manchester Jewish Telegraph* (this newspaper also has copies in Leeds, Liverpool and Glasgow with genealogical notice sections), *Manchester Jewish Gazette*, *The Watchman* (Newcastle area) and newspapers from Leeds.

6.4 Guildhall Library (Manuscript Section)

Aldermanbury, London, EC2P 2EJ
Tel: 020 7332 1862
E-mail: manuscripts.guildhall@corpoflondon.gov.uk
Website: *http://ihr.sas.ac.uk/gh*

The Manuscript Section of the Guildhall Library is the local record office for the City of London although it does not hold the archives of the City of London Corporation itself, which are separately administered. Its holdings date from the eleventh century and include ecclesiastical and probate records, records of City wards and parishes and of around eighty of its ancient livery companies, military and taxation records, and records of several foundations that originated in the

City of London, for example Christ's Hospital School and Trinity House. In keeping with its location, it also holds considerable business and commercial archives, including those of the London Stock Exchange, Lloyd's of London, the London Chamber of Commerce and numerous banks, insurance companies, stockbrokers and merchants. The Guildhall Library itself is famous for its collection of trade directories, which is said to be the best in the country. In the region of 1,500 Jewish businesses were listed in Pigot's Alphabetical Directory of London in 1836. It is also very useful for its collection of old insurance policies, which contain a wealth of genealogical information.

Further reading
Richard Harvey, *A Guide to Genealogical Sources in Guildhall Library*, 4th edn, 1998

6.5 Huguenot Library

University College London, Gower Street, London, WC1E 6BT
Tel: 020 7679 5199 (by appointment only)
E-mail: library@huguenotsociety.org.uk
Website: *www.huguenotsociety.org.uk*
The Huguenot Library at University College London was formed by the amalgamation of the libraries of the French Hospital (1718) and the Huguenot Society (1885) and deposited in 1957. A collection of around 6,000 books, many periodicals, and a great series of manuscripts, prints and engravings may be seen. The bulk of the printed book collection covers the whole range of Huguenot studies, from major histories to printed family records, dating from the mid-nineteenth century onwards.

The Huguenot Library is housed within the Special Collections of UCL Library, 140 Hampstead Road, London, NW1: note, this is NOT a postal address – see above for postal address and contact details.

6.6 Jewish Genealogical Society of Great Britain – Library and Resource Centre (JGSGB)

For details about the Library, Resource Centre and the Society, please *see 1.7.2.*

6.7 London School of Jewish Studies (formerly Jews' College)

Schaller House, 44a Albert Road, Hendon, London, NW4 2SJ
Tel: 020 8203 6427   Fax: 020 8203 6420
E-mail: info@lsjs.ac.uk
Website: *www.lsjs.ac.uk*

The London School of Jewish Studies, previously known as Jews' College, was founded in London as a rabbinical seminary in 1852. Today, the London School of Jewish Studies is primarily a modern orthodox Yeshiva but its library has the most extensive collection of books on Judaica and Hebraica in Europe (over 70,000 volumes) and as such is a good source of information for genealogists.

The library also has United Synagogue seat-holder's books for 1875, 1899 and 1910. These contain the names and addresses of all the synagogue members in London United Synagogues. In addition, there is a complete set of *Jewish Chronicles* (commencing 1841) in original form.

6.8 Society of Genealogists (Library)

14 Charterhouse Buildings, Goswell Road, London, EC1M 7BA
Tel: 020 7251 8799   Fax: 020 7250 1800
E-mail: genealogy@sog.org.uk and library@sog.org.uk
Website: *www.sog.org.uk*

The Society of Genealogists has the largest family history library in the UK. It holds copies of family history sources, finding aids, indexes and unique research materials. Its library also has free Internet access to some major genealogical websites.

The library is the foremost genealogical library in the British Isles with a large collection of family histories, civil registration and census material, and the widest collection of parish register copies in the country (over 9,000). They are arranged with local histories, poll books and directories, other topographical material, and the publications of county records and archaeological societies. Sections relate to the professions, schools and universities, the services, religious denominations, the peerage and heraldry, and to British citizens living abroad, in the Commonwealth and USA. Boyd's Marriage Index covers some 2,600 parish registers with nearly 7 million names: a general card index contains some 3 million references: there are about 6,000 rolls of microfilm (including Scottish civil registration indexes) and the International Genealogical Index (IGI) on both CD-ROM (Family Search with over 200 million names) and fiche.

The unique manuscript collections relating to families include several significant collections of notes on Jewish families compiled by Isobel Mordy, Albert Montefiori Hyamson, Thomas Colyer-Ferguson and Ronald D'Arcy Hart.

6.9 University College Jewish Studies Library

Arnold Mishcon Reading Room, University College, Gower Street, London, WC1E 6BT
Tel: 020 7679 2598   Fax: 020 7679 7373
E-mail: library@ucl.ac.uk
Website: *www.ucl.ac.uk/library/jewish.htm*

The Arnold Mishcon Reading Room is part of the main UCL library. It is on the second floor, reached from a staircase off the landing by the library entrance stairway. It is open to the general public for research by arrangement – identification is required.

6.9.1 COLLECTIONS
The two main book collections, Mocatta and Hebrew, are interfiled into a single subject sequence on the shelves, so all material on a particular topic can be found in one location. Other collections include Altman and Abramsky.

6.9.2 ANGLO-JEWISH PAMPHLET COLLECTION ON MICROFICHE
This collection, produced by the Jewish Theological Seminary of America, contains 442 rare pamphlets, covering Jewish History in England from the late sixteenth to the late nineteenth centuries.

6.9.3 THE WILLIAM MARGULIES YIDDISH LIBRARY
The Library covers a wide range of subjects, amongst them language and linguistics, history, folk literature, theatre, biography, with particular strength in literature and criticism.

6.9.4 REFERENCE BOOKS AND PERIODICALS
Jewish encyclopaedias, dictionaries and bibliographies are kept in the Jewish Studies Library. As with the book collections, the two sequences of periodicals, previously the 'Hebrew' and the 'Mocatta', are now interfiled. The sequence contains a full set of the *Transactions of the Journal of the Jewish Historical Society of England*. There is a full set of the *Jewish Chronicle*, which is the oldest Jewish periodical still in existence, having first appeared in 1841. Because of the fragile nature of the original paper copies, the *Jewish Chronicle* is only available for consultation on microfilm for the period 1860–1959.

6.9.5 ILLUSTRATIONS
The library has a collection of illustrations on Jewish subjects, portraits and photographs. Some items can be traced in the card catalogue, and a hand list is available in the Jewish Studies Library. Items must be consulted in the Manuscripts and Rare Books Reading Room. This is by arrangement with the Jewish Studies Librarian or Library Archivist.

6.10 Wellcome Library

Reader Services Department
Wellcome Library, 210 Euston Road, London, NW1 2BE
Tel: 020 7611 8722   Fax: 020 7611 8369
E-mail: library@wellcome.ac.uk
Website: *http://library.wellcome.ac.uk*
The Wellcome Library was founded on the collections formed by Henry Solomon Wellcome (1853–1936). Today, through its collections and services, it provides insight and information to anyone seeking to understand medicine and its role in society, past and present. More than 30,000 readers visited the library in 2006. With over 600,000 books and journals, an extensive range of manuscripts, archives and films, and more than 100,000 pictures, they are one of the world's major resources for the study of medical history.

6.11 Wiener Library *(see also 12.2.3)*

4 Devonshire Street, London, W1W 5BH
Tel: 020 7636 7247   Fax: 020 7436 6428
E-mail: info@wienerlibrary.co.uk
Website: *www.wienerlibrary.co.uk*

Regional Libraries and Archives

6.12 Birmingham Central Library & Archives

Chamberlain Square, Birmingham, B3 3HQ
Tel: 0121 303 4511   Fax: 0121 233 4458
E-mail: central.library@birmingham.gov.uk
E-mail: archives@birmingham.gov.uk
Archives: Tel: 0121 303 4217
Website: *www.birmingham.gov.uk/libraries*

Birmingham Central Library is one of the largest and most important public libraries in Europe. Books on the history of the Birmingham Jewish Community have been published over the past twenty years and copies are available from public libraries across the West Midlands as well as in the Local Studies Library. The Local Studies and History Service on the sixth floor of Birmingham Central Library has an extensive range of material for tracing families in the Birmingham area but a more limited amount for families originating from elsewhere. (*See the section on 'genealogy' for a list of the library's holdings.*)

6.13 Liverpool Records Office and Local Studies Service

Liverpool Central Library, William Brown Street, Liverpool, L3 8EW
Tel: 0151 233 5817   Fax: 0151 233 5886
E-mail: recoffice.central.library@liverpool.gov.uk
Website: *www.liverpool.gov.uk*

According to the JewishGen website 'Archival Resources section', the Jewish archives held at the Liverpool Central Library go back to 1780. They house book-lets and listings of almost all of the Jewish cemeteries and who was buried there, with details on date of burial, name, address of person at death, age and plot number. Most of the documents are written in English or Yiddish. They cover almost all the Jewish cemeteries from the early eighteenth century to the present day. However, these are not allowed to be taken from the library archives. They may only be viewed on the premises and only with special permission and by appointment. In order to do this you will need to write to the Office of the Chief Rabbi explaining why you wish to view the records. If he agrees, you will receive a letter granting you permission. Photocopies are not permitted, but you may take photographs.

Catalogues of the archives held at Liverpool Record Office are now available via the Internet (including the Jewish Archive Collection). The catalogues can be accessed via *www.liverpool.gov.uk*; from here go to A-Z of council services and then to Archives. This will take you to the home page, and by clicking on the link you can then search the catalogues.

6.14 Bodleian Library

University of Oxford, Broad Street, Oxford, OX1 3BG
(Contact Admissions office in advance of visit)
Tel: 01865 277180   Fax: 01865 277105
E-mail: admissions@bodley.ox.ac.uk
Website: *www.bodley.ox.ac.uk*

The Bodleian Library is the main research library of the University of Oxford. It is also a copyright deposit library and its collections are used by scholars from around the world. Hebrew books have been in the Bodleian Library since its opening in 1602. Unusually, the interest in Hebrew stems directly from the library's founder, Sir Thomas Bodley, who was deeply learned in both biblical and post-biblical Hebrew. He shared the view of most scholars of his time that Hebrew was the parent of all languages, and consequently viewed the collecting of Hebrew books as the most important aspect of his library's work. Even today, the library selects and acquires hundreds of the latest Hebrew books from Israel every year, so that there is an unbroken tradition of collecting Hebrew books from Bodley's time to the present.

All the Hebrew books, both manuscript and printed, fall under the jurisdiction of the Department of Oriental Collections, and should be consulted in the Oriental Reading Room at the Central Bodleian Library.

6.15 Leopold Muller Memorial Library

Oxford Centre for Hebrew and Jewish Studies, Yarnton Manor, Yarnton, Oxfordshire, OX5 1PY
**Tel: 01865 377946 (by appointment)   Fax: 01865 375079
E-mail: muller.library@ochjs.ac.uk
Website: *www.ochjs.ac.uk/index.html***

The Leopold Muller Memorial Library is housed in two converted stone barns at Yarnton Manor. As a bibliographic centre the Leopold Muller Memorial Library provides an unparalleled resource for bio-bibliographic and literary-historical research. The library's complete catalogue is available online. Recent additions to the collection include the Library of Rabbi Dr Louis Jacobs, the Loewe Collection and the Coppenhagen Library.

The main constituents are the Kressel and Elkoshi collections, comprising over 35,000 volumes in Hebrew and over 7,000 volumes in western languages. The collections cover the full range of Hebrew and Jewish studies, with special focus on Hebrew literature of the nineteenth and twentieth centuries, Haskalah, modern Jewish history, Zionism, and Israel. The Kressel collection includes a biographical and historical archive of some 500 box files of Hebrew newspaper and periodical cuttings on 12,000 Jewish personalities and on the early *Yishuv* in Palestine, as well as representative samples of the Hebrew and Yiddish press. There is also a collection of Jewish books and *Yizkor* books.

6.16 Hartley Library (Parkes Library)

University of Southampton, Highfield, Southampton, SO17 1BJ
Tel: 023 8059 2180   Fax: 023 8059 3007
E-mail: libenqs@soton.ac.uk
Website: *www.soton.ac.uk/library/about/hl/index.html*

The Parkes Library is part of the Special Collections Division on Level 4 of the Hartley Library. It contains a major Jewish archive. Members of the public may use the collection for reference purposes. The Parkes Library originated as the private collection of the Reverend Dr James Parkes (1896–1981), an outstanding semitophile, and was transferred to Southampton University Library in 1964. The library now amounts to over 20,000 items, and includes material on the history of Jewish communities, the history of Palestine and the development of Zionism, Arab-Jewish relations, Jewish-Christian relations, anti-semitism and the Holocaust. For the Jewish Studies Section website, see *www.soton.ac.uk/library/subjects/jewishstudies/archives.html*.

Museums

6.17 Imperial War Museum (Holocaust Exhibition) *(see also 12.5.1)*

Lambeth Road, London, SE1 6HZ
Tel: 020 7416 5320   Fax: 020 7416 5374
E-mail: mail@iwm.org.uk
Website: *www.iwm.org.uk*

6.18 Jewish Museum

Raymond Burton House, 129–131 Albert Street, London, NW1 7NB
Tel: 020 7284 1997   Fax: 020 7267 9008
E-mail: admin@jmus.org.uk
Website: *www.jewishmuseum.org.uk*

Founded in 1932, the Jewish Museum had its initial home in the Jewish communal headquarters at Woburn House in Bloomsbury. Over the years, the museum has built up one of the world's finest collections of Jewish ceremonial art. As one of Britain's oldest minority communities, Jewish people have played an important role in the development of multicultural Britain. The Jewish

Museum tells the story of Jewish people in Britain since medieval times, and explores the fascinating and diverse culture and traditions that many generations have brought from all over the world.

6.19 London Museum of Jewish Life

The Sternberg Centre, 80 East End Road, London, N3 2SY
Tel: 020 8349 1143   Fax: 020 8343 2162
E-mail: enquiries@jewishmuseum.org.uk
Website: *www.jewishmuseum.org.uk*

The London Museum of Jewish Life was founded in 1983 as the Museum of the Jewish East End. While the East End has remained an important focus, the museum has expanded to reflect the diverse roots and social history of Jewish people across London. It also developed an acclaimed programme of Holocaust and anti-racist education.

This museum has social history collections. These include a small library, an oral history archive with some 400 tape-recorded memories. There is a photographic archive (with over 15,000 images) and a wide range of documents and artefacts. In addition, there are Holocaust education and social history exhibitions. The museum arranges tours of the East End of London from May to September.

In conjunction with the museum, the Jewish Genealogical Society of Great Britain holds regular family history workshops. These offer a fantastic opportunity to consult standard texts, swap information and get advice from experts and are especially designed to help the beginner to Jewish genealogy or those who are stuck. It is advisable to take your family tree with you. Further information may be obtained from the museum.

6.20 Museum of London

150 London Wall, London, EC2Y 5HN
Tel: 0870 444 3852 (local call rates)
E-mail: info@museumoflondon.org.uk
Website: *www.museumoflondon.org.uk*

The Museum of London is the world's largest urban history museum with 1.1 million objects and Europe's largest archaeological archive. The museum's collections are its richest resource. They contain the material remains of London's vast, complex past and are an inspirational source of knowledge. Material includes items from Jewish firms and articles related to Jewish trade, in particular a large collection of early twentieth-century wine-making and bottling equipment from the kosher wine cellars of M Chaikin & Co. of Brick Lane. This collection also includes printed ephemera and other material related to Dr Bernard Homa, a community leader and trustee of the synagogue in Fournier Street, Spitalfields.

Material from other firms of Jewish origin includes a quantity of items relating to Jo Lyons, including a 'Corner House' shop front and a 'Nippy' uniform. The costume collection has many items related to the Jewish East End tailoring trade. The museum also has the surgery contents from Dr Barber, a Czechoslovak doctor of Jewish origins who settled in London after the Second World War.

The 2D collections contain several nineteenth-century images of synagogues, Jewish soup kitchens and other charitable initiatives. The *Woodin Album* contains photographs of the late nineteenth-century Jewish community in Whitechapel.

The oral history collection is particularly rich in material relating to Jewish London, from the 1890s onwards. This includes the tapes recounting memories of the Rothschild Buildings and an East End tenement largely inhabited by Jewish families.

6.21 Library and Museum of Freemasonry, The United Grand Lodge of England *(see also 16.9)*

6.22 West Midlands Police Museum

Sparkhill Police Station, 639 Stratford Road, Sparkhill, Birmingham, B11 4EA
Tel: 0845 113 5000 or Mobile: 07973 869916
E-mail: d.a.cross@west-midlands.police.uk
Website: *www.westmidlandspolicemuseum.co.uk*
The alien registers for Birmingham are held at this museum and cover the period 1914–19.

6.23 Manchester Jewish Museum (MJM)

190 Cheetham Hill Road, Manchester, M8 8LW
Tel: 0161 834 9879   Fax: 0161 834 9801
E-mail: info@manchesterjewishmuseum.com
Website: *www.manchesterjewishmuseum.com*
The museum was originally a Spanish-Portuguese synagogue which was built in 1874, but it has been a museum since 1984. The downstairs synagogue has been fully restored to its original splendour with lavish Moorish décor and fine stained glass. Upstairs is a permanent exhibition of Manchester's Jewish history. Heritage Trail walks round areas of Jewish historical interest take place once a month, from March to October.

An appointment is required to access the archives. These include oral histories, an un-indexed photographic archive, and limited synagogue registers and records: see the following for details.

6.23.1 PROBATE RECORDS
The MJM has access via Rosalyn Livshin to a partial national Jewish name index to the probate records for 1858–1920. The date makes it possible to apply for the will from the probate registry.

6.23.2 CENSUS
The years 1841–81 have been searched for Jewish names and information. These are handwritten and are stored on loose leaf sheets with a handwritten index.

6.23.3 CITY DIRECTORIES
The MJM holds details of all identifiable Jewish names extracted from the local directories up to 1850. The Manchester and Salford directories of streets, names and trades are available on microfilm at the Central Reference Library.

6.23.4 SCHOOL ADMISSION REGISTERS
These exist for the Jews' School for 1874–1940. Southall Street School for 1896–1930 and Waterloo Road School for 1913–55. These schools were located in the densely populated Jewish areas of Cheetham and Strangeways. Admission registers also exist for schools on the outskirts of these areas. The registers are held at the Archives Department of the Central Reference Library: Jews' Infant School Register (boys' and girls' birthdates) for 1891-1901, (photocopy), entry 1899–1904; Jews' Infants School Register (boys' and girls' birthdates) for 1898–1905, entry 1904–08; Jews' Girls School Register (girl's birthdates) for 1860–73 (photocopy), entry 1876–84; Jews' Boys School Register (boys' birthdates) for 1860–73 (photocopy), entry 1874–82.

6.23.5 NEWSPAPERS
The MJM has an index of newspaper cuttings but the cuttings themselves are stored off site. It also holds a Jewish name index for the *Manchester City News* for 1875–1923. The paper itself is on microfilm at the Central Reference Library as are the other local newspapers such as the *Manchester Evening Chronicle*, *Manchester Evening News* and the *Manchester Guardian*.

6.23.6 BIRTH RECORDS
The MJM houses the birth registers of the Spanish and Portuguese Synagogue for 1874–1929 and the birth register of midwife Dora Black for 1913–34; the

Central Reference Library contains the counterfoils of birth certificates for 1859–72 and the circumcision registers of Prosper Mesod Zicree for 1873–1912.

6.23.7 Marriage records

The MJM holds an index to all Jewish marriages in the city of Manchester for 1900–50; a copy of the Register of Marriages for the Spanish and Portuguese Synagogue for 1873–1908; the marriage register of the New Kahal Chassidim, Waterloo Road, 1929-52; an index to miscellaneous *Ketubot* which are housed off the premises.

The Central Reference Library houses a number of marriage records including those of the North Manchester Synagogue for 1895–1915; Great Synagogue counterfoils for 1854–1911; the New Synagogue 1924–7.

6.23.8 Naturalization records

The MJM has access via Rosalyn Livshin to a naturalization index of Jewish names for the whole country for 1780–1914.

6.23.9 Burial records

The MJM has copies of the burial register of Prestwich Jewish Burial Ground for 1873–4 and of the Burial Register of the North Manchester Spanish and Portuguese Section of Urmston Cemetery.

6.23.10 Biographical records

These include files on individuals and families; oral history interviews, summaries and selected transcripts; and biographical material from the Photographic Collection.

6.23.11 First World War

Here you can consult the British Jewry Book of Honour.

6.23.12. Philanthropic Records

The MJM has a copy of the Book of Relief of the Old Hebrew Congregation for 1848–51.

6.23.13 Miscellaneous

This includes the Workers Circle Membership Register for 1912–54.

6.24 Greater Manchester Police Museum and Archives

57A Newton Street, (corner with Faraday Street), Manchester, M1 1ET
Tel: 0161 856 3287   Fax: 0161 856 3286
E-mail: police.museum@gmp.police.uk
Housed in a former police station built in 1879 and in use until 1979, this museum tells the story of policing in Manchester.

6.24.1 ALIENS REGISTRATION
Aliens were required to register with the police from 1914, and to give details of birth place, address, date of birth, particulars of family and so on. Second World War enemy alien slips at the Public Record Office are only for aliens who were not interned. The museum holds alien registers for Salford only for 1916–60. There is a public restriction on the registers of seventy-five years due to their sensitive nature, but requests can be made to the Police Museum or the MJM for information pertaining to an individual's family. The MJM has an index. An appointment is necessary to view the Alien Registration Books.

6.25 Jewish Community of the South Manchester suburb of Didsbury 1891–1914

(see 3.1.28 for further details)

6.26 The Holocaust Centre, Beth Shalom

(see 12.5.2)

Chapter 7

MARRIAGE AND DIVORCE

In the introduction to this book I noted Anthony Joseph's comment that Hardwicke's Marriage Act of 1753, subsequently amended by the Marriage Act of 1823, exempted Jews and Quakers from its provisions. Although the English courts appear to have always recognized Jewish marriages as being valid in law, no interest was taken by the authorities in enforcing a system of registration before the introduction of the national civil registration system. Thereafter, duly certified synagogues maintained their registers and sent in their returns to the Registrar General in precisely the same manner as other denominations. The Orthodox Jewish community itself demanded for a long time that all Jewish marriages, whether of their own members or of other Jewish groupings (such as the Reform community), be recorded via the Orthodox returns and sent on to the Registrar General. This gave rise to considerable ill-feeling between different segments of the Jewish community in that the Reform and Progressive elements were dissatisfied with having their affairs supervised by the Orthodox community. It was also possible, under this system, for the Orthodox grouping to refuse to sanction a marriage if they did not approve of the religious provenance under which it was solemnized or, more particularly, if they were not satisfied that one or both parties to the marriage were Jewish. From time to time the problem was resolved by Act of Parliament, empowering the Registrar General to authorize non-Orthodox groupings to hold a licence for solemnizing marriages. It may be noted, in passing, that many of the secular counterpart marriage certificates submitted to the Registrar General were signed by one or both of these participants making a mark (usually a circle). It has been suggested that this proves considerable illiteracy amongst the immigrant Jewish population, but a more likely explanation is that Hebrew would have been the language spoken and written by the Jewish bride and/or groom, and Hebrew script was not allowed by the English civil authorities on secular documentation. It has also been noticed that frequently the bride and groom appeared to have been living at the same address at the time of a marriage. This has given rise to speculation that many such marriages had, in fact, taken place under Jewish religious law before the secular ceremony was also performed. Here, too, this is unlikely, and usually such religious and secular marriages followed each other closely. The explanation for only one address being given was that it reduced the cost of the exercise if the statutory fee for civil marriage involved only one parish.

Nevertheless, the possibility of a Jewish marriage having been solemnized in accordance only with Jewish religious practice is very real and explains why, in many cases, no marriage for a couple can apparently be identified in the secular registers. Jews who used this tradition would satisfy their religious conscience and would feel perfectly comfortable living with each other as man and wife in such circumstances. The Registrar General did not approve of the practice, however, since it undermined the concept of civil marriage as part of the fabric of society. No duly licensed synagogue sanctioned such marriages, and if connivance at the practice was discovered, penalties were applied. This notwithstanding, the practice was quite widespread, being known as *stille chuppah* (silent marriage) and of course, resulted in a lack of any centrally indexed documentation that can be used to track down the participants.

In Jewish religious custom, a marriage is valid if solemnized in the presence of two religiously fit Jewish witnesses and if a *Ketubah* (pl. *Ketubot*, marriage contract) is then issued to the bride. Before the secular civil registration system, the *Ketubah* may be the only evidence of a marriage, and if the supporting documentation copies have not been kept with the synagogue, it may be impossible to discover any further details. The practice of lodging a duplicate copy of the *Ketubah* with the archives of the Congregation issuing it became widespread only after the latter part of the nineteenth century.

7.1 Jewish marriages

The majority of Jewish weddings in the UK are held on a Sunday, although the ultra orthodox tend to hold them during the week. Weddings may be held on any day of the week apart from during the Sabbath (*Shabbat* שבת), which runs from sunset on Friday until sunset on Saturday, or on any major Jewish festival. In addition, couples tend to avoid the period between the festivals of Passover (*Pesach* פסח) and Pentecost (*Shavuot* שבועות) which is known as the *Omer* (this is marked by the counting of the forty-nine days from the second day of *Pesach* until the day before *Shavuot*) as this is a sad time in the Jewish calendar. During this period, people refrain from parties involving music and dancing. However, on the 33rd day of the Omer (18 Iyyar), this ban is lifted and is known as *Lag B'Omer* (בעמר לֿ״ג), when all festivities are permitted.

7.2 Requirements of a Jewish marriage

Jewish marriages under the auspices of an Orthodox synagogue may only take place if both the bride and the groom are of Jewish parentage. The Office of the Chief Rabbi checks this by asking the couple to provide a copy of their parents' *Ketubah* and marriage certificate. These will show that the parents were married in an Orthodox synagogue.

According to Rabbinical Jewish Law, Judaism descends through the mother. This means that in a mixed marriage, should the mother be Jewish then the children of that marriage will be recognized by the Jewish authorities as being Jewish too. However, if the children are from a marriage where the mother is a Gentile and the father is Jewish the children will not be recognized as being Jewish. Should the non-Jewish parent have previously converted to Judaism under Orthodox supervision, then the children will be recognized as being Jewish.

7.3 Marriage authorization

The authorization by the *Beth Din*, or rabbinical court, is issued once the couple have been interviewed and the *Beth Din* has established that they are both halachically Jewish. Unless the authorization issued from the *Beth Din* and the certificate (or licence) issued by the superintendent registrar are both received by the secretary for marriages prior to the date of the wedding, the marriage may not take place. The only difference between early marriage authorizations and the ones issued today are that today the forms include the date of birth and place of birth of both parties.

Example of marriage authorization certificate.

Through the United Synagogue, you can order online copies of marriage authorization certificates for marriages which took place under the auspices of the Office of the Chief Rabbi before 1906. In order to order a marriage authorization certificate they require the following information:

- full name of bridegroom
- full name of bride
- year of marriage between 1880–1906
- your full name
- your full postal address
- e-mail address or contact telephone number.

The cost of one certificate will be £20 for United Synagogue members and £30 for non-United Synagogue members.

7.4 Marriage Registers

All synagogues hold two marriage registers. When both registers are full, one must be delivered to the superintendent registrar of the district in which the synagogue is situated. The other must be kept with the other registers and records of the synagogue. Should a synagogue permanently close, this should be notified to the Registrar General in order that he or she may give instructions regarding the marriage register books. The United Synagogue holds marriage registers for some congregations.

7.5 Marriage ceremony

In the Jewish tradition a marriage takes place under a canopy called a *chuppah* (חופה). The top is made of white satin, usually with Hebrew inscriptions around the sides. It is supported by four poles. Some couples have the ceremony outside (as this was the custom in the Middle Ages). The *chuppah* symbolizes the home in which the couple will begin their married life. The bride circles the bridegroom seven times. The number seven is generally considered a number of good fortune in Judaism, and is attributed to various sources. One source cited for the custom is the verse from Jeremiah, 'for the Lord hath created a new thing in the Earth, a woman shall compass a man' (Jeremiah 31:21). Every Jewish wedding ends in the bridegroom breaking a glass. There are a number of explanations for this tradition, one of which is that we remember sadness at the height of personal joy.

7.6 *Ketubot* (plural) (marriage contract)

Since the Talmudic period (324–638 CE) the *Ketubah* (כתובה) has been an essential requirement of marriage; the document becomes the property of the wife and she is not allowed to live with her husband unless the *Ketubah* is in her possession. The United Synagogue holds *Ketubot* for some congregations.

A Ketubah, *or marriage contract.*

The terms and conditions of the *Ketubah* are set out in the *Mishnah* (משנה) (early third century CE).

The *Ketubah* is the marriage contract which was introduced into the Jewish wedding ceremony about 2,500 years ago. It was written in Aramaic, as this was the language of the Jews at the time. Today, the *Ketubah* is still written in Aramaic and read at the marriage service, an abstract of which is generally printed on the reverse in English.

The *Ketubah* is a legal document that declares the obligations a man has to his wife, including financial security to which she is entitled according to biblical law. The *Ketubah* is, in effect, a one-sided contract entered into by a bridegroom and is intended to safeguard a woman in the case of divorce.

If a person does not have the *Ketubah* of a deceased relative and needs the details of the marriage, then the Marriage Authorization Department of the Office of the Chief Rabbi should be contacted. It is important that the husband's name, wife's maiden name and the marriage date is given. Once this information has been received, then a copy of the authorization (not *Ketubah*) will be issued.

In recent years, the United Synagogue has asked synagogue secretaries for marriages to keep duplicate copies of *Ketubot*. However, if the synagogue has not got a copy, the United Synagogue will only reissue a *Ketubah* if the husband applies to Rabbi Dr Julian Shindler (and makes an appointment to see him.) If you require a copy of, say, your great-grandparent's *Ketubah*, this is not possible as the United Synagogue will not reissue *Ketubot* from couples who have died, because the *Ketubah* is no longer valid.

7.6.1 The *Ketubot* digitization project

This aims to create a worldwide registry of *Ketubot* in public and private collections throughout the world. Based on the collection of the Jewish National and University Library with over 1,200 items, the project contains *Ketubot* originating from dozens of different countries, and covering a time period of over 900 years. See the project's website (*http://jnul.huji.ac.il/dl/ketubot*).

7.7 Bevis Marks Synagogue marriage records

Bevis Marks Synagogue is the oldest Jewish house of worship in Great Britain. It is situated in the City of London, just off the ancient thoroughfare of Bevis Marks.

The marriage records are published in two volumes, for 1686–1901, and may be purchased from:

The Archivist, Spanish and Portuguese Synagogue (Lauderdale Road Synagogue), 2 Ashworth Road, Maida Vale, London, W9 1JY
Tel: 020 7289 2573   Fax: 020 7289 2709

7.8 Marriage Certificates

Jewish marriages result in two pieces of paper, the *Ketubah* and the marriage certificate.

7.8.1 The National Archives (TNA)

TNA has records of marriages dating from 1 July 1837. Indexes up to 1983 are compiled alphabetically in yearly quarters by date of registration. Marriages are registered in the quarter in which the marriage took place. From 1984 the indexes are arranged in alphabetical order for the full year. The entry contains the month and year of registration under the column headed 'reg'. The first two digits 01–12 indicate the month and the last two digits indicate the year. The marriage indexes for March quarter 1912 onwards show the surname of the second party to the marriage alongside the name and surname of the other party.

The example below of a marriage certificate indicates that the bride could not read or write as against her name is shown an 'O' and next to it is written 'the mark of Nancy Ellis'. Note: Jews who could not read or write did not want to put the mark of a cross, so they used a circle instead.

7.8.2 The General Registry Office (GRO)

GRO indexes are also available on microfiche/microfilm. You can search these in many libraries, county record offices and family history societies in England and Wales. A small fee is sometimes charged for this service. Note: marriages will always appear in the GRO indexes because reporting them was the responsibility of the registrar – unlike births, which around 1900 were the responsibility of the parents, who sometimes did not report them.

Barnett–Ellis marriage certificate.

7.9 Marriage notice books

The Tower Hamlets Local History Archives hold marriage notice books for Stepney from 1926 and for Bethnal Green for 1837–78 and 1920–65. These contain marriage applications, which give the date, names of couple, marital status, profession, age, address, length of residence in the UK, place of intended marriage.

7.10 Marriage announcements

The British Library Newspaper Library has a full set of *Jewish Chronicles* and they may be viewed 10 a.m.—4.45 p.m. Monday–Saturday. Entry is restricted to those over the age of 18 and proof of identity will be required. (Access to the building is from 9.30 a.m. but not to the library until 10 a.m.)

7.11 International Genealogical Index (IGI)

If you need to trace marriage records before July 1837, you would be well advised to start with the IGI index. This index includes marriages worldwide. The indexes to the British Isles cover the period from the beginning of registration to 1875. There are some drawbacks to the IGI: its coverage is not complete, since some registers have not been included, and there is no guarantee that the registers which have been covered are included in full. Most of the entries are taken from parish records from around the sixteenth century. The IGI does not include records of deaths and burials.

7.12 Divorce

In the Jewish religion, a civil divorce is not sufficient to dissolve a Jewish marriage. It is important that a couple arrange for a *Get* גט (*Sefer Keritut* ספר כריתת – 'book of severance/cutting off' as referred to in the Talmud (תלמוד)/Deuteronomy 24:1-4) when they divorce. Unless the husband gives his wife a *Get*, they will remain married according to Jewish law and therefore neither party may remarry.

The reason behind this is that if a married woman commits adultery before she has her *Get*, the couple will never be able to marry each other in a religious ceremony. If the couple choose to have children, within the Jewish religion, these children will be considered illegitimate.

If the couple are halachically Jewish, in order to ensure that the *Get* is recognized throughout the Jewish world it must be obtained from an Orthodox *Beth Din* (בית דין).

Further reading
Harold and Miriam Lewin, *Marriage Records of the Great Synagogue, London 1791–1885* (POB 253, Jerusalem 91002).

Chapter 8

DEATH AND BURIAL

In the Jewish religion, a person is buried as quickly as possible after death, where possible within a twenty-four-hour period. The only delay is when a person dies on the Sabbath or on a Jewish festival or if a post-mortem is required. The tombstone should be erected within a period of one year from the date of death. It is customary for the family, relatives and friends to attend the memorial stone setting ceremony at the cemetery, when prayers for the deceased are said. The date set for the stone setting usually appears in the *Jewish Chronicle*. This is particularly useful for the genealogist as it will tell them where the person is buried.

Jewish customs

It is the custom for the next of kin to have a week of mourning, known as *Shivah* (שבעה). Not so much these days, but, say 100 years ago, it was customary to put an announcement in the *Jewish Chronicle* thanking relatives and friends for their sympathy during the week of mourning. Sometimes the names of the family are included, so this is another source whereby you might find further information about the family in question.

Locating a person

The minimum information needed to locate a person is their name and date of death. If for some reason you do not know the actual date of death but think it could be within a range of, say, two to three years either side of a particular date, then it would be well worthwhile looking through the death indexes held at the National Archives (*see 8.1.1*).

8.1 Where do I start?

8.1.1 The National Archives (TNA)

The indexes at TNA (previously held at the Family Record Centre) are filed for each quarter. The death indexes for March quarter 1866 to March quarter 1969 show the age at death. From the June quarter 1969 onwards the deceased's date of birth is shown. A death that occurred in one quarter of a year may have been registered in a subsequent quarter and will therefore be found in a later index. When looking up a name, do take note of alternative spellings. If you are lucky and find who you are looking for, you will be able to order a copy of his or her death certificate at the same time.

Other death records include still-births registered in England and Wales since 1 July 1927; deaths at sea since 1 July 1837; deaths in aircraft since 1949 relating to deaths occurring in any part of the world in any aircraft registered in Great Britain or Northern Ireland, plus service records of deaths among members of HM Forces. Entries in the army registers date mainly from 1881, although some records extend back as far as 1761. Royal Air Force returns commenced in 1920 and the Royal Navy returns commenced in 1959.

8.1.2 General Registry Office (GRO) Indexes

These are available in many libraries, county record offices and family historical societies in England and Wales on microfiche/microfilm. A small fee is sometimes charged for using this service.

General Registry Office, PO Box 2, Southport, Merseyside,
PR8 2JD
Tel: 0845 603 7788
E-mail: certificate.services@ons.gsi.gov.uk
Website: *www.gro.gov.uk*

8.2 UK death certificates

Death certificates in the UK give information on the date and place of death, name, sex, age, occupation, cause of death, name and address and relationship of informant. Please note: UK death certificates do not give a place of burial, unlike many American ones.

I have located the death certificate at the National Archives but I still do

not know where my ancestors are buried – what should I do next?
The United Synagogue probably covers the bulk of burials, and the website of the United Synagogue Burial Society (*www.unitedsynagogue.org.uk*) has a search facility for checking the grave location of your loved ones. However, to use this you must have the full name of the person, where they are buried and the year they were buried. To get to the relevant section on the website, go to the top of the page, click on 'Support Services', then on the drop-down list 'Find your Family'.

8.3 Sephardi records

Bevis Marks Synagogue publishes its historical records. The burial registers run from 1733 to 1918 for the Novo (New) Cemetery. (Birth, marriage and circumcision records are published too.)

8.4 Classes of people

In order to give an additional idea of where your ancestors might be buried, Sephardi burials were generally for Iberian or Dutch Jews and the United Synagogue was for old-established families' pre-1900. Eastern European immigrants tended to use the Federation and Adath Yisrael cemeteries.

8.5 Cemetery opening times

Most cemeteries are open every day, including bank holidays, but are closed on Saturdays and the Jewish festivals. During the winter months, most cemeteries will close a couple of hours before Shabbat. Please take this into account when planning your visit. In addition, the older cemeteries may not have any staff on site. It is advisable, for safety purposes, not to visit any cemeteries alone. Also check opening times before your visit.

8.6 Photography at cemeteries

Please check with the office staff before taking photographs. Some cemeteries are quite happy to allow you to do this, whereas others are not. If you are allowed to do so, please bear in mind where you are and allow time for reflection at each grave. Remember, some graves may not have been visited for many years and you may be the last person visiting the grave for many more years to come.

Note: look around to see if there is someone near visiting a family grave or perhaps a funeral or a stone setting is taking place. If so, please do not take your photograph whilst they are close by.

8.7 International Jewish Cemetery Project

The International Association of Jewish Genealogical Societies (IAJGS) Cemetery Project mission is to catalogue every Jewish burial site throughout the world. See *www.iajgs.org* or *www.jewishgen.org/cemetery*.

Willesden United Synagogue Cemetery war memorial.

8.8 Jewish newspapers

8.8.1 *Jewish Chronicle* (JC) *(see 16.7)*

8.8.2 *Gentleman's Magazine*

This magazine was a monthly magazine (first publication January 1731) published in London in the eighteenth, nineteenth and early twentieth centuries. The Bodleian Library in Oxford has page images for the first 20 volumes, from 1731–50. These may be viewed at *http://onlinebooks.library.upenn.edu/serials.html*.

The magazine published quite a number of articles relating to the death of Jews. An index listing these has been compiled under the title of 'Jewish Obituaries in the *Gentleman's Magazine* 1731–1868'. This has been published in the Miscellanies Part IV of the Jewish Historical Society of England in 1942.

Further reading

Rosemary Wenzerul, *Jewish Ancestors: A Guide to Jewish Genealogy in the United Kingdom* (Jewish Genealogy Society of Great Britain, 2006: ISBN 0-9537669-7-7). This book lists all the cemeteries under town headings.

Rosemary Wenzerul, *Jewish Ancestors: A Guide to Reading Hebrew Inscriptions and Documents* (Jewish Genealogy Society of Great Britain, 2005: ISBN 0-9537669-6-9). This book will help you to read the Hebrew inscriptions on the gravestones in Jewish cemeteries as well as other related documents.

Chapter 9

READING GRAVESTONES

Many people find it difficult to interpret the symbols and Hebrew inscriptions on headstones. Below are various icons and symbols used on headstones. In addition, there are details of the Hebrew alphabet with numerical values, the months of the Hebrew year and days of the month and numbers in Hebrew and English.

9.1 Reading gravestones

9.1.1 Interpreting symbols on graves

Jewish iconography, as well as the symbols which Jews borrowed from other traditions, has been adapted for this use. Over the next few pages is a key to some of the most common icons, with descriptions to help interpretation.

Grave marker showing a tree with broken limbs, representing a life cut short.

Masonic symbols are quite common among older Jewish graves since many were active in such local fraternal orders.

The Torah scroll, Tor ah (תורה), is G-d's teaching to the Jewish people. It is the first five books of the Jewish Bible, Genesis, Exodus, Leviticus, Numbers, and Deuteronomy. It is written on parchment on scrolls and read from them in the synagogue. The Torah then is represented on grave markers as a scroll.

(Above) *The lion is the symbol of the tribe of Judah. Certain Jewish names related to the Lion (e.g. Ari, Judah, Leib), so this symbol may be a reference to the name of the deceased.*

(Right) *Grave marker showing a veil, symbol of the* tallit *(טלית) or prayer shawl widely used on Victorian markers. Another device was an urn with such a veil draped over it, resembling a Jewish man bent in worship.*

The Ten Commandments (Exodus 20:1–17) are represented on grave markers as two tablets.

The Deer is a reference to such Jewish names as Hirsch, Herschel, Zvi. The deer is a symbol of the tribe of Naphtali, Jacob's sixth son whose mother was Rachel's handmaid (Genesis 30:7–8).

The crown is a symbol of the re-establishment of the kingdom of Judah. There are also three essential crowns: *Keter Malchut* (כתר מלכות), the crown of Kingship; *Keter Torah* (כתר תורה), the crown of Torah; and *Keter Kehunah* (כתר כהונה), the crown of priesthood.

The offering box symbolizes the charity of the deceased or may refer to his office as treasurer.

The symbols on the Jewish graves in Commonwealth War Grave cemeteries tend to be the Star of David as well as the insignia of the deceased's regiment. In addition to Commonwealth War Grave cemeteries these may also be found on war graves in local cemeteries.

THE MAGEN DAVID (STAR OF DAVID)
This is the most popular motif and is the traditional symbol of Judaism.

THE SHELL DESIGN
This design is chosen by people wishing to enhance the appearance of their chosen memorial but who do not wish to incorporate any religious symbolism on their memorial.

COHEN HANDS
This represents the position of the Cohen's hands whilst blessing the community in synagogue. This may only be used if the deceased was a male Cohen.

JUG & BASIN (LEVI)
This symbol represents the duty that the Levites perform when washing the hands of the Cohanim before they bless the community. This may only be used if the deceased was a male Levite (Levi).

HANDS & CANDLES
This represents the woman's duty in the household of lighting the Shabbath candles and is also a symbol of light. This may only be used on a memorial which is to be erected for a woman.

MENORAH (CANDELABRA)
This is the ancient symbol of Judaism, representing the menorah of the temple and has been used on memorials for the last 2,000 years.

Some common signs used on gravestones. Reprinted with permission of A Elfes Ltd.

א	ב	ג	ד	ה	ו	ז	ח	ט	י	כ ך
1	2	3	4	5	6	7	8	9	10	20
ל	מ ם	נ ן	ס	ע	פ ף	צ ץ	ק	ר	ש	ת
30	40	50	60	70	80	90	100	200	300	400

The Hebrew alphabet with numerical values.

9.2 Numerical values

Each letter in the Hebrew alphabet has been designated a numerical value. Final letters have the same value as non-final letters. For example, if you wished to write the number 31, the Hebrew letters would be *lamed, aleph* (לא). There are a couple of exceptions. Numbers ending in 15 or 16 would be written as *yod-hay* (10+5) and *yod-vav* (10+6), but these letters spell out the name of G-d and for religious reasons are not used. Instead, by convention, *tet-vav* (9+6 =טו) and *tet-zayin* (9+7 = טז) are always used. However, the number 18 for example, *yod-chet*, uses the same letters as the word for life *chet-yod*. So instead of יח, you may see חי. The order of writing the letters is generally irrelevant to their value since the numerical values are added up to produce a total. Note: thousands, if written, are designated by a single quote next to the letter. א׳ = 1000, ה׳ = 5,000.

A double quote between the last two letters signifies a year. This example תש״ו represents 706, and the year (5)706. (Thousands are usually omitted when writing Hebrew dates.) In addition, when the thousands are omitted, the following three Hebrew letters may appear after the date: לפ״ק = לפרט קטן. If the thousands are included, the following Hebrew letters are shown לפ״ג = לפרט גדול.

9.3 The Jewish calendar

The Jewish calendar is a lunar calendar. The lunar year is usually eleven days shorter than the solar year. There are normally twelve months in the Jewish year and each month is based on how long it takes the moon to orbit the earth. Some months have twenty-nine and others thirty days. A leap year has thirteen months. The thirteenth month is called *Adar II / Adar Sheni* (אדר שני/אדר בי). There are seven leap years in every cycle of nineteen years.

English Months	Hebrew Months		Days of the month			
Sept/Oct	תשרי	Tishri	1	א	16	טז
Oct/Nov	חשון	Cheshvan	2	ב	17	יז
Nov/Dec	כסלו	Kislev	3	ג	18	יח
Dec/Jan	טבת	Tevet	4	ד	19	יט
Jan/Feb	שבט	Shevat	5	ה	20	כ
Feb/Mar	אדר	Adar	6	ו	21	כא
Mar	אדר בי	Adar II	7	ז	22	כב
Mar/Apr	ניסן	Nisan	8	ח	23	כג
Apr/May	איר	Iyar	9	ט	24	כד
May/Jun	סיון	Sivan	10	י	25	כה
Jun/Jul	תמוז	Tammuz	11	יא	26	כו
Jul/Aug	אב	Av	12	יב	27	כז
Aug/Sep	אלול	Elul	13	יג	28	כח
			14	יד	29	כט
			15	טו	30	ל

The Hebrew months.

Further reading

Rosemary Wenzerul, *Jewish Ancestors: A Guide to Jewish Genealogy in the United Kingdom* (Jewish Genealogical Society of Great Britain, 2006: ISBN 0-9537669-7-7). This book gives details of all the cemeteries in the UK and lists them under town headings.

Rosemary Wenzerul, *Jewish Ancestors: A Guide to Reading Hebrew Inscriptions and Documents* (Jewish Genealogical Society of Great Britain, 2005: ISBN 0-9537669-6-9). This book will help you to read the Hebrew inscriptions on the gravestones in Jewish cemeteries as well as other related documents.

Chapter 10

EXTENDING YOUR FAMILY HISTORY

Genealogy is an interest, which may be left for years then resumed at any time in the future. To ensure that future generations inherit as much information as possible, it is important to bring your family history to life. To do this, you will need to research the social history of your family. This is the study of your family's everyday lives. In this chapter, I hope you will find sufficient information to help you do this.

If you have children, now is a good time to involve them in helping you to obtain additional information. It is so important to get them interested while they are still able to speak to the older members of their family. If for some reason they are loath to speak to you, it is amazing how the 'generation gap' works, so a grandchild speaking to a grandparent usually works wonders.

If you are unable to obtain information from your family about a particular year, perhaps the year your grandfather was born, for example 1873, then you might like to follow an idea I took from the *Ancestry Weekly Journal*, which suggested that you type into Google '1873' or 'the year was 1873' to see what comes up. To my amazement there were a considerable number of items that could be used to describe 'the scene' at the time and which would be ideal to add interest to your family history.

10.1 Where to begin

If you break your family history down into appropriate sections, you can focus on your research and perhaps involve other people to help you. The object of including so many headings below is to provide a wide selection of ideas, some of which you may not have thought of, and which you might wish to consider. The sections should be arranged into some order, either chronological or alphabetical. As I have said earlier, be as accurate as possible with dates, names and events and, most of all, add a bit of humour to your stories in order to make them more interesting.

10.1.1 Family

If the family you are researching is very large, with numerous children, break it down into sections showing each child and their families separately. If possible, include photographs in each section and as many stories as you can for each one. Should you wish to expand, include separate files on 'associated families' (in alphabetical order by surname).

10.1.2 Births

Include photographs of the family as babies (dated on reverse); the *Jewish Chronicle* or other regional newspaper insertion; baby words; their first lock of hair; birthday parties held over the years – where they were held and who came to them; any birth certificates you acquire (file in alphabetical order by surname). You might ask the grandparents to write about the pleasure of seeing their first grandchild and his/her progression to adulthood.

10.1.3 Bar Mitzvah/Bat Mitzvah

Use photographs of the event, the invitation, the table plan, memorabilia, and so on. You might want to include details of the synagogue, what portion was read and of course the *Jewish Chronicle* or other regional newspaper insertion/ photograph if appropriate. Encourage your children to write about the events of the day, as so much revolves around the youngsters on these occasions.

10.1.4 Marriages

Include the name of the synagogue where the wedding took place; the names of the persons who officiated; photographs of the wedding (if a group, name them from left to right); invitations; menus; marriage certificates (in alphabetical order by surname of bridegroom); *Ketubot*; table plan; memorabilia, and so on.

10.1.5 Graves

If you visit a cemetery, take photographs of the graves. If you do not know the grave location, ask the cemetery office and record it. Note the inscription on the grave; the *Jewish Chronicle* or other regional newspaper insertion; and date of stone setting. When visiting a cemetery, allow time for reflection at each grave to remember the life of your relative.

10.1.6 School

Describe the school location. It may still exist by name but may have moved several times. Include school reports, certificates, group photos of your class (name them, including teachers). If you know the name of a particular school, it might be worthwhile having a look at the school log books. These describe the school day activities, education provided, teaching methods and the names of those pupils who caused problems, for example those who were absent. They also include details of the lessons and textbooks used. They were first intro-

Lady Eleanor Holles School for Girls, Mare Street, Hackney, London, c.1918

duced around the 1850s. If the records are not logged at the London Metropolitan Archives, they may still be held by the school or by the local record office; however, they are often closed to inspection for thirty years after the last entry. Note the degree you obtained and the degree ceremony, and dated photographs of the occasion and your memories of the day.

10.1.7 Employment

What was the occupation of the family? Did they own a business? Did they have employees or did they work for someone else? Include any relevant documents, for example, curriculum vitae, contract of employment, job description, achievements and promotions and, of course, any colleagues. Most of these documents will include a date, which will help, should you wish to make contact with the firm concerned.

10.1.8 The family at war

Note photographs of your family in uniform; where and when they served; the name of their regiment and service number if known; medals they won; call-up papers; letters they wrote to loved ones; stories of what happened to them during the war and of course what happened to the civilian members of the family, plus any other memorabilia they may have.

10.1.9 Property

If you know where the family lived (whether it is in the UK or abroad) you may have pictures of the property. Photocopy a map of the area and highlight the road. If you have reduced the map ensure to say so and state the source so that the map can be found in the future. If the property still exists you could either photograph it yourself, or if it happens to be on the market, contact the estate agent for details. Make lists from birth, marriage and death certificates and from other sources of the addresses of your family and the dates they lived there. Build up a picture of their lives. Remember that a large number of Jews owned public houses both in the East End and West End of London. Although it was a hard life, it gave large families the accommodation they required and they would always have food. It is well worth while looking to see if the pub still exists by entering the name in a search engine such as Google. For information on house and building societies, see *www.cyndislist.com/houses.htm*. If you wish to find out more about your house this is an excellent website to point you in the right direction.

Thanks to the combined efforts of *Ancestry.co.uk* and British Telecom (*see 3.1.6 and 5.10*) you will now be able to do an online search of British phone books for 1880–1984, by name, year and county. This will enable you to trace where your ancestors once lived and to build a more detailed picture of your family history. The total collection contains in excess of 250 million names. The 430 London books alone (which include the counties of Surrey, Hertfordshire, Essex, Kent and Middlesex) contain over 72 million names.

10.1.10 Maps and gazetteers

Now that you have found the property where your ancestors lived, it is time to have a look at old maps and gazetteers.

For information on European gazetteers, have a look at *www.familysearch.org*. Look under Jewish Family History Resources, then Jewish Genealogy Research Outline and view page 25 Gazetteers. Alan Godfrey Maps is one of a number of firms who sell maps (see *www.alangodfreymaps.co.uk*). They have an excellent selection of old ordnance survey maps of the UK. The East End of London and the City of London maps are of particular interest to Jewish family historians and are very reasonably priced at £2.50 each plus p&p. They also have an online map store. Other resources include Multimap (*www.multimap.com*) and Streetmap (*www.streetmap.co.uk*), both of which will help locate any present-day addresses.

The British Cartographic Society's website links are well worth viewing: see *www.cartography.org.uk*.

Further reading
Dave Obee, 'Using Maps and Gazetteers in Your Research' (this may be seen at *http://feefhs.org/maps/obee-1.html*). Dave Obee of Victoria, British Colombia, is the owner of Genealogy Unlimited, which specializes in maps of Eastern Europe.

10.1.11 Freemasonry

Were some of your family free-masons? If so, include photographs and details of their Lodge and so forth. If you need more information, you can write to the United Grand Lodge of England. Unfortunately, they take quite a while to reply!

10.1.12 Family sayings

Most families have their own sayings, some quite expressive! List them and explain what they mean, examples of when they were used and whose expressions they were.

A silver collar jewel worn by senior Masonic officers during ceremonies. The square (an angle of 90 degrees) is referred to in masonic ritual as an important tool used by ancient masons and is used to signify various elements of good moral and humanistic behaviour in Freemasonry.

10.1.13 Hobbies

If your ancestor had an unusual hobby or was actively involved in sport, there could be certificates, newspaper write-ups or photographs of the occasions.

10.1.14 Family recipes

Almost all families have recipes, which have been handed down from generation to generation. It is

Potato gateau – a family recipe!

important for these to continue through future generations, so make the effort to write them out. If the finished recipe looks very appetizing and is decorated, photograph it. Remember to record the origin and the name of the person who gave it. If you have a photograph of the person, include this as well.

10.1.15 Newspapers

Newspapers have been in circulation since the early seventeenth century. They tend to be an extremely underused resource for obtaining genealogical information, which is a great shame as they have so much to offer.

Make a note of the birth, marriage and death announcements relating to your family and ensure you record the date they appeared in the *Jewish Chronicle*, regional and local Jewish newspapers. In addition, look through the papers for obituary columns, as these will give far more information than the above short announcements and very often provide personal and family details.

10.1.16 Memorabilia

Start to collect memorabilia, whether in the form of badges, plastic cards, brochures showing the produce or fashion prices in a specific year and so on. Look at photographs of yourself and of your ancestors and see if there are any family resemblances.

10.1.17 Photographs

If the photographs you have are in the family album and the negatives are not available, to avoid fading or damage I would suggest copying, scanning or re-photographing them. This can be done in situ without spoiling the album. Ensure you include the name, date, event and location against each photograph. Have a good look at the clothes worn in the photographs and look at the back of very old photos: these often give the name of the photographer

Note the name and address of the photographer.

and the address of the studio. Trade directories may tell you when they were in business. For further details go to *www.cyndislist.com/clothing.htm*. An excellent website for dating Victorian and Edwardian photographs is the Roger Vaughan Personal Collection (*www.cartes.freeuk.com*).

10.1.18 Correspondence

Keep all correspondence relating to the research you have done in alphabetical or date order (by surname) for future reference. Always make a note of where the information came from so you can return to it at a later date. From time to time, refer back to old correspondence since you may well have missed a vital entry, which at the time did not mean much to you but now that you have more information, may be relevant.

10.1.19 References

Make a separate file of any references you acquire. For example, if you visit the Public Record Office or Newspaper Library, ask at reception for the leaflets giving details of the organization and the opening times and so forth and keep on file for future reference. Always date these references so when they become out of date you can replace them.

10.1.20 Website for children

Genealogy for Kids – Kids Turn Central
www.kidsturncentral.com/links/genealogylinks.htm
If you have children, this website has some very attractive printable family history tree forms with teddy bears as well as a picture of a tree, to which information may be added. This is a good way to encourage your children to begin their family history. There is also a section to help your child begin his or her family history.

10.1.21 Conclusion

However you decide to bring your family history to life, it is important to be as accurate as possible with the information you hold and, most important of all, to share the information you have with other researchers. The more names and information you can swap with others the more interesting and exciting genealogy becomes, since the more information you receive the more links, friends and relations you are likely to make along the way. Do remember to give credit to the researchers who have provided you with the information.

There is no race to finish your tree: this is a never-ending interest. You may not be able to go any further backwards in time, but future generations are continuing and it is for future generations that your family history is aimed, so ensure that you enjoy what you are doing and make your family history as interesting, humorous and informative an interest as possible.

Advice, precautions and preservation

10.1.22 Digital photographic repairs

Digital retouching of photographs will remove any damage to your photographs and preserve them for future generations. This may be done in Photoshop, or, if you feel you are not skilled enough to do this, photographs may be taken to someone who specializes in this process. (*Examples are shown below*).

10.1.23 Computers

It is worthwhile keeping copies of everything on your computer, as well as the original documents. Digitizing documents and photographs is a good way to preserve them, and gives you a freely accessible database. Copies can be distributed quickly and cheaply to other members of your family. That way, you keep your handling of the originals down to a minimum, which in itself should give them longer life and you have a digital version that can be preserved almost indefinitely as long as you make sure you transfer it every time you get a new computer! There are books available on the subject, so it might be worth your while visiting your local library to ask for their help.

A family photograph before restoration.

The same photograph, repaired by Nigel Fidlan.

10.1.24 Back-up your data

Most important of all, remember to periodically back-up all the data on your computer. This can be done on a writable CD or DVD or external hard disc drive. In addition, if you wish to use your data on a friend's system, why not invest in a memory key which just plugs into a USB port. Some Internet service providers (ISPs) offer a service to back-up data for their customers on the ISP servers. Whatever system you decide to use to back-up your system, DO NOT leave the disc next to your PC. Keep your back-up in a different room and leave a copy with a friend or relative. If you had a fire, flood or lightning strike, both the computer and the data would be destroyed and you would have lost all your work.

10.1.25 New technology

It is important to update the method of archival storage of computer records as technology changes.

10.1.26 Computer viruses

If you use your computer for e-mail or to access the Internet, or you receive data in computer readable format, it is essential that you invest in anti-virus and fire-wall computer software to protect your computer and your valuable data. There are a number of reputable suppliers of such software, but you must ensure that you have a subscription that permits you to download regular updates, as new versions of viruses are found daily.

It is suggested that you download updates at least once a week. Virus check any data given to you in a computer readable format before loading it onto your computer. Do not open attachments sent with e-mails unless you know the sender and expect the attachment from them. Even then, ensure that the attachment is scanned before being opened.

10.1.27 Plastic document covers

Ensure you purchase acid-free plastic document covers that will not lift the print from your documents. These should be made of polyester not from PVC (or branded as Melinex) as the covers deteriorate and become highly acidic and will eventually destroy the documents you are trying to preserve. However, polyester covers cost several times more than the PVC ones.

10.1.28 Laminators

Laminating your documents or photographs will NOT help preserve them. If the document is very fragile the heat from the lamination process may damage it further. Once a document or photograph is laminated it can never be removed. In addition, documents can still deteriorate within the lamination.

Further reading

Rosemary Wenzerul, *Jewish Ancestors: A Guide to Organising Your Family History Records* (Jewish Genealogical Society of Great Britain, 2005: IBSN 0-9537669-4-2).

Rosemary Wenzerul, *Genealogical Resources within the Jewish Home and Family* (Federation of Family History Societies, 2002: ISBN 1-86006-148-6).

Chapter 11

THE ARMED FORCES

W hether Jewish or not, most records for the armed forces in the UK are held at the National Archives (*see 4.5.4*) or museums such as the Imperial War Museum or various regimental museums. However, there are a number of Jewish military museums both in London and around the world which hold records and memorabilia and would be well worth contacting.

11.1 The Jews and the First World War: 1914–18

The following details are taken from the British Jewry Book of Honour. During the Great War, 60,000 Jews are recorded as having served in one or other branch of His Majesty's Forces. Eighty per cent of those serving were in fighting units. Some 3,000 Jews gave their lives for Britain in the war, 334 officers and 2,666 non-commissioned officers and men. Nearly 7,000 were wounded. Jews lie with their comrades-in-arms of other faiths in every war cemetery in Flanders, Gallipoli and elsewhere. In addition, Jews gained 5 VCs, 49 DSOs, 263 MCs, 85 DCMs, 329 MMs and 865 other honours and distinctions. The Commander of the Australian Forces during the latter part of the war, General Sir John Monash, was Jewish.

German war memorial websites

The purpose of the website *www.denkmalprojekt.org/en.htm* is to memorialize the names of the dead and to collect, archive and make publicly available, particularly for use by genealogists, inscriptions from war memorials of the

German and Austrian armies. The term 'war memorial' should be read broadly, as it is meant to include memorial books (such as the RJF Memorial Book, which memorializes Jewish First World War casualties of the German armed forces), lists of casualties kept by municipalities and grave inscriptions from war cemeteries, particularly where they are located far from home. The collection is limited to monuments to fallen soldiers of the German and Austrian armed forces of all wars. The website is arranged by country and region and covers the Federal Republic of Germany, Austria and the former German eastern territories.

On the *www.germanjewishsoldiers.com/memorial.php* website are references to monuments located in other countries and a roll of honour commemorating the 12,000 German Jewish servicemen killed in action in the German Army, German Navy and German Colonial Forces in the First World War.

11.2 The Jews and the Second World War: 1939–45

The following information was taken from the AJEX Military Museum's website (*www.ajex.org.uk/warRecord.htm*), with permission from Martin Sugarman, assistant archivist.

Of the estimated Jewish population of 400,000 in the United Kingdom in 1939, something like 70,000 Jewish men and women served during the Second World War in the British Armed Forces, of whom 14,000 were in the Royal Air Force, and 1,500 in the Royal Navy. The figures are those of men and women actually contacted by Jewish chaplains or whose names have appeared in authentic and checked nominal rolls. They do not include Dominion personnel or the 30,000 men and women who voluntarily enlisted in the British Forces in Palestine.

British Jews bore their full share of the war in every quarter of the globe in the operations on land, on sea and in the air, as indeed they continued to do in the Korean conflict, Malaya, Kenya, the Falklands and other theatres of war. About 10,000 Jewish refugees, who had sought refuge in Britain from Hitlerism just before the war, enlisted in Alien Pioneer companies, and so proved their worth, trust and martial qualities that many were transferred to first-class fighting battalions, some becoming commandos and paratroopers, and not a few being commissioned and awarded decorations.

Palestine Jews served with the Royal Navy, Army and Royal Air Force. They were in France in 1940, in the campaigns in Greece and Crete, in the Western Desert, and again in Europe. The Jewish Infantry Brigade Group, commanded by Brigadier E F Benjamin CBE, fought in Italy, and its members won four MCs, seven MMs, two OBEs, four MBEs, two American awards, and seventy-two Mentions in Despatches. Polish Jews served with the Army and RAF. Many fought in the Battle of Britain and at Monte Cassino.

11.2.1 Killed or died on service

British and Palestinian Jews killed/died in service during the Second World War.

Army	1,865
Royal Navy (including Royal Marines)	202
RAF	889
Palestinian Jews	694

Second World War Awards to Jewish Servicemen

Mentioned in Despatches	1,081	DFC	184
MC	162	MBE	160
MM	151	BEM	92
OBE	91	DFM	64
DSO	43	Bar to DFC	42
DSM	35	DCM	30
CBE	28	Croix de Guerre	36
Other foreign Awards	30	DSC	25
Certificate of Gallantry	31	GM	19
AFC	19	US Bronze Star	12
Colonial Police Medal	8	American DFC	7
CB	6	US Legion of Merit	6
Legion D'Honneur	8	Bar to DFM	5
Air Force Medal	5	GC	3
CGM	3	Bar to DSC	3
VC	3	Air Efficiency Award (AEA)	3
Bar to MC	2	Bar to MM	3
American DSO	1	DSM and Bar	1
MSM	1		

11.3 The Jewish Brigade

The Jewish Brigade was an infantry fighting unit in the British Army, composed of 5,000 volunteers from the British Mandate of Palestine. They fought on the side of the Allies against the Axis Powers, Nazi Germany, Fascist Italy and the Empire of Japan. Their insignia was a white central vertical band with a central yellow hexagram (six-pointed linear star) known as the *Magen David* centred between two equal vertical blue bands.

Further reading
Morris Beckman, *The Jewish Brigade: An Army with Two Masters, 1944–45* (Spellmount, 1998).

11.4 The Palestine Brigade

During the Second World War, the Palestine Brigade of the British Army fought in Europe. It was composed exclusively of Jewish volunteers.

11.5 Jewish Legion (Zion Mule Corps)

The Jewish Legion was the name for five battalions of Jewish volunteers established as the British Army's 38th to 42nd (Service) Battalions of the Royal Fusiliers. The initial unit, known as the Zion Mule Corps, was formed in 1914–15 during the First World War, when Britain was at war against the Ottoman Turks.

11.6 Jewish Military Union (Żydowski Związek Wojskowy ŻZW)

During the Second World War, the ZZW (created by members of the Betar Zionist Youth and Revisionist movements) was an underground resistance organization of around 250 people, active in the Warsaw Ghetto. It was part of a major organization (with around 750 people) known as Zydowska Organizacja Bojowa (ZOB), Polish for Jewish Fighting Organization.

Cyril Baron Benjamin BEM.

Army chaplain's record card. The Jewish Military Museum holds 70,000 chaplain's cards for the soldiers who served in the Second World War. (© Permission of Martin Sugarman, Assistant Archivist, Jewish Military Museum)

11.7 Army chaplains

Since the end of the eighteenth century, there have been chaplains in the British Army. The Jewish Military Museum holds 70,000 chaplain's cards for the soldiers who served in the Second World War. The example of the chaplain's card above shows that Cyril Baron Benjamin was awarded the British Empire Medal (BEM) in the New Year Honours January 1946. His photograph appears above.

The Jewish Committee for H.M. Forces, 25 Enford Street, London, W1H 2DD
Tel: 020 7724 7778   Fax: 020 7706 1710
E-mail: jmcouncil@btinternet.com

This committee is officially recognized by the Ministry of Defence to appoint Jewish chaplains and to provide for the religious needs of Jewish members of HM Forces.

11.8 Newspapers

If a member of your family was killed on active service or their names were in the New Year Honours List, then it is well worth looking up the newspapers of the time. In the case of Cyril Baron Benjamin, because he was Jewish, details of his British Empire Medal (BEM) appeared in the *Jewish Chronicle* as well as in the national press.

11.9 The National Archives (TNA)

Military records may be found at the National Archives, Ruskin Avenue, Kew. Simon Fowler, editor of The National Archives' family history magazine, has recently written a book entitled *Tracing Your Army Ancestors*. This is a comprehensive introduction to researching army history, which shows how to trace the careers of individual soldiers from 1760 to the present day. In addition, it explains army organization and regimental histories as well as information on all the major archives and museums including the National Archives.

11.10 Commonwealth War Graves Commission (CWGC)

2 Marlow Road, Maidenhead, Berkshire, SL6 7DX
Tel: 01628 634221   Fax: 01628 771208
E-mail: general.enq@cwgc.org
Website: *www.cwgc.org*

As I have said above, Jews fought in both the First and Second World Wars and since, and lie with their comrades-in-arms of other faiths in many war cemeteries. Some 1,700,000 men and women of the Commonwealth Forces died in the two world wars. Of these, the remains of 925,000 were found, and their graves are marked by a headstone. Where the remains were not found, the casualty's name is commemorated on a memorial. There are war graves in some 150 different countries; mostly in the 2,500 war cemeteries and plots constructed by the Commission. In addition, the CWGC holds details of 60,000 civilian casualties of the Second World War. There are also war graves in many civil cemeteries, churchyards and Jewish cemeteries throughout the world.

11.11 War memorials

Many synagogues and cemeteries have war memorials. The Imperial War Museum has compiled a United Kingdom National Inventory of War Memorials (*see 3.1.34*).

11.12 Then and now

It would be wonderful for future generations to see a photograph of their relative in uniform and then fifty years later, a very proud ex-serviceman wearing his medals.

Left: *Barry Molen (Vandermolen) in 1943. 7014452, 1st Battalion, London Irish Rifles, 56th London Division (wounded on Anzio beachhead).*

Right: *Barry Molen in 1993.*

11.13 Jewish war poets

There were four famous Jewish war poets, namely Isaac Rosenberg, Siegfried Sassoon, Frank Templeton Prince and, rather less well known, Uri Zvi Grinberg – although Sassoon and Prince were not technically Jewish, since Judaism is passed through the female lines.

11.13.1 Isaac Rosenberg

Isaac Rosenberg was born in Bristol in 1890 and seven years later the family moved to London. He was the son of Jewish immigrants. Rosenberg enjoyed painting and also wrote poetry. Due to ill health, he emigrated to South Africa. In early 1915 he returned to England and in October 1915 joined the Bantams. This was a special battalion for men who were too short to be accepted into other regiments. He was then sent to the Somme and was on the Western Front for the next couple of years. He was killed in 1918. His body was never found. In 1922, his friends arranged for his poems to be published.

11.13.2 Siegfried Lorraine Sassoon

Siegfried Sassoon was born in England in 1886. His father was Jewish but his mother was a Catholic. Therefore, as mentioned above, technically Siegfried was not Jewish. He enjoyed hunting, cricket and poetry. He was a captain in the Royal Welch Fusiliers and when, early in the war, his brother was killed at Gallipoli, he took the news very badly, taking revenge by involving himself in brave, sometimes suicidal actions against the Germans and winning the Military Cross. This revenge worked its way into his poetry. His later war poetry attacks the entire nature of war and those who profited by it. He died in 1967.

11.13.3 Frank Templeton Prince

Frank Templeton Prince was born in the mining town of Kimberley, South Africa, on 13 September 1912 and died on 7 August 2003, aged 90. His father Harry Prinz was Dutch-Jewish and his mother Scottish. During the Second World War he worked as an Intelligence Officer at Bletchley Park and in the Middle East. In 1954, he composed what came to be his best-known poem, 'Soldiers Bathing'.

11.13.4 Uri Zvi Grinberg

Uri Zvi Grinberg was born in Galicia in 1896. His early poems, both in Hebrew and Yiddish, were published in 1912. In 1915 he joined the Austrian Army and fought during the First World War. In 1917 he deserted and returned to Lvov, where he witnessed the Polish pogroms against the Jews in 1918. Grinberg's poetry expresses the love, hate, fury and joy of a stormy spirit.

11.14 Jewish war artists

11.14.1 Abram Games

Abraham Gamse was born in 1914 in the East End of London. He was the son of Joseph Gamse, a photographer. In 1926 Joseph anglicized the family name by changing it to Games. In 1939 Abraham Games was called up to the army. After six months as a private, he was given the designated role of draughtsman. In 1942 he was promoted to captain and given the title of Official War Artist. He was appointed the government's official war poster designer.

11.14.2 David Bomberg

David Bomberg was born in Birmingham in 1890 and died in 1957 in Spain. He trained as a lithographer before studying painting in London at the Westminster and Slade School of Art. During the Second World War he was an Official War Artist. In 1917 the Canadian authorities commissioned him to paint a picture to celebrate an operation in which sappers successfully blew up a salient of the German defences at Saint-Eloi near Arras.

11.15 Military Museums

11.15.1 UK: AJEX Jewish Military Museum/Association of Jewish Ex-Servicemen and Women (AJEX)

Harmony Way, Hendon, London, NW4 2BZ
Tel: 020 8202 2323   Fax: 020 8202 9900
E-mail: headoffice@ajex.org.uk
Website: *www.ajex.org.uk* (visits by appointment only)

The museum commemorates the unique contribution to the armed forces of the Crown made by British Jews who have loyally served their country. AJEX wishes to ensure that the contribution of Jewish servicemen and women in many campaigns dating from the eighteenth and nineteenth centuries to the present day is not forgotten.

In addition to a Jewish Book of Honour from the First World War, the museum has a computerized Record of Honour which allows visitors to search for their own details or those of any relatives who were involved in the armed forces from the Second World War to the present day. The Annual AJEX Remembrance Parade takes place at the Cenotaph in London on the Sunday following National Remembrance Sunday.

At the time of writing, the museum is compiling a Roll of Honour of all Jews who served in the Fire Service or as Firewatchers in the Second World War. Contact Martin Sugarman at the above address or e-mail (martin.sugarman@ westking.ac.uk).

11.15.2 USA: National Museum of American Jewish Military History

1811 R Street NW, Washington DC, DC20009
Tel: 202 265 6280   Fax: 202 462 3192
E-mail: nmajmh@nmajmh.org
Website: *www.nmajmh.org*

The National Museum of American Jewish History's collection is made up of over 10,000 artefacts. The collection includes objects from nearly every American military conflict, with the bulk of the collection relating to the Second World War. In addition, it contains substantial materials related to American Jewish military history from the Civil War to the present. The collection includes original photographs, letters, diaries, films, military documents, newspapers and manuscripts related to Jewish–American military history. The archives also contain materials relating to the history of US Jewish war veterans (1896 to the present).

11.15.3 Canada: Jewish Canadian Military Museum

788 Marlee Avenue, Suite 308, Toronto, Ontario, M6B 3K1
Tel: 416 781 6344
E-mail: office@jcmm.ca
Website: *http://jcmm.ca*

The history of the Jews in the Canadian military and of their exploits and experiences dispels the myth that Jews have not contributed their share in the

Canadian Armed Forces. This includes the Boer War (1899–1902), First World War (1914–18), Second World War (1939–45), and the Korean War (1950–3), as well as Canada's ongoing peacekeeping activities throughout the world. Since 1759, when it is documented that Jews fought with General James Wolfe, members of the Jewish community have participated in every significant conflict that has involved Canada. In the past century, Canadian Jewry, along with the rest of the Allies, under the shadow of the Holocaust, helped liberate Europe. The museum pays everlasting tribute to the thousands of Jewish men and women in the Canadian military who helped foil the Nazis' plans for killing the remaining Jews in the death and labour camps.

11.15.4 National Army Museum

Royal Hospital Road, Chelsea, London, SW3 4HT
Tel: 020 7730 0717   Fax: 020 7823 6573
E-mail: info@national-army-museum.ac.uk
Website: *www.national-army-museum.ac.uk*
Almost everything you wish to know about tracing army records is shown on this website.

Records of soldiers serving between 1921 and the present day may be obtained from

The Army Personnel Centre, HQ Secretariat Historical Disclosures, Mail Point 400, Kentigern House, 65 Brown Street, Glasgow, G2 8EX

Note: information will only be released to next of kin and a fee of £30 is charged.

Army records

Registers of the gentleman cadets of the military colleges at Woolwich and Sandhurst are held at

The Royal Military Academy, Sandhurst, Camberley, Surrey, GU15 4PG
Tel: 0127 663344

11.15.5 Royal Air Force Museum

Grahame Park Way, Hendon, London, NW9 5LL
Tel: 020 8205 2266 (general information)
E-mail: london@rafmuseum.org
Website: *www.rafmuseum.org.uk*

The whole collection comprises several hundred thousand objects ranging in size from aircraft to lapel badges, and spanning more than a century of aviation history. In addition, a total collection of well over 200 aircraft, over 100 full-size aircraft from all over the world are displayed under cover on the historic site of the original London Aerodrome. These include the legendary Spitfire and Lancaster Bomber.

RAF records

Records for the Second World War are held at

The Ministry of Defence at RAF Insworth, Gloucester, GL3 1HW
Tel: 01452 712612
Indexes to RAF deaths from 1939–48 are held at the National Archives at Kew.

Royal Navy Records

The National Archives at Kew have an index to the naval dead for both the First and Second World Wars and hold a register of reports of deaths from 1939–48 of naval ratings. For service records for 1928–38, contact

The Ministry of Defence, Royal Naval Records, CS (R)2A,
Bourne Avenue, Hayes, Middlesex, UB3 1RF
Tel: 020 8573 3831 / ext. 341/342

For service records after 1938, contact

The Ministry of Defence, HMS Centurion, Grange Road, Gosport,
Hampshire, PO13 9XA

Personal service records of officers are held for seventy-five years after their date of entry into the service. Records of those who served before 1909 are at the Public Record Office. Only written enquires from next of kin are accepted.

11.15.6 Royal Naval Museum

H.M. Naval Base, Royal Historic Dockyard, Portsmouth, PO1 3NH
Tel: 023 9272 7562
Website: *www.royalnavalmuseum.org*
The Royal Naval Museum is one of Britain's oldest maritime museums. The museum is located in Portsmouth Historic Dockyard, alongside three great ships, HMS *Victory* (Admiral Lord Nelson's flagship at the Battle of Trafalgar in 1805), *Mary Rose* (Henry VIII's flagship, which sank in 1545), and HMS *Warrior* 1860 (Britain's first ironclad battleship). The museum does not hold any personnel records in their collections. For information on where to obtain records and information about personnel, please see the *useful sources* page.

11.15.7 Military badges

The website *www.militarybadges.org.uk* is useful for identifying military badges.

Further reading
Henry Morris (compiler), Gerald Smith (editor), *We Will Remember Them* (AJEX) and its sequel, *The Addendum*, gives comprehensive details of those who died and all who received decorations.

Henry Morris, *History of AJEX* (AJEX, 2000).

Simon Fowler, *Tracing Your First World War Ancestors* (Countryside Books, 2003).

Simon Fowler, *Tracing Your Second World War Ancestors* (Countryside Books, 2006).

Simon Fowler, *Tracing Your Army Ancestors* (Pen & Sword, 2006).

Recommended website: *www.regiments.org*. This is a general site (not Jewish), with a wealth of information about the regiments of the British Army. You might also Google 'Martin Sugarman', as he has written an enormous amount about this subject, or look at the AJEX Jewish Military Museum's website, which lists his publications.

Chapter 12

THE HOLOCAUST

The Holocaust is an extremely specialized subject, so I hope that the following will give you an insight into where to obtain information. Some 6 million European Jews as well as homosexuals, gypsies, people with physical or mental disabilities and Jehovah's Witnesses were killed or tortured in concentration camps during the Second World War. In addition, many innocent citizens were killed just for their beliefs or for helping their Jewish neighbours.

12.1 Concentration camps, killing centres and ghettos

Soon after the Nazis came into power in 1933 concentration camps were set up. The main ones then were Buchenwald, Dachau, Flossenbürg, Ravensbrück (for women) and Sachsenhausen in Germany, and Mauthausen in Austria. During the Second World War they increased in size and numbers, the best-known ones being Auschwitz, Belzec, Bergen Belsen, Gross Rosen, Izbica, Kulmhof (Chelmno), Lodz, Maidanek, Minsk, Riga, Sobibor, Stutthof, Theresienstadt and Treblinka. For further details see the Holocaust website *www.JewishGen. org/ForgottenCamps.*

12.2 Where to start finding a missing relative believed to be a victim of the Holocaust

12.2.1 The 1939 German Census

Lists are catalogued by the name of the town and may therefore be of little use, unless the town where the person lived at that time is known. Some named individuals may still have been able to emigrate after the census was taken in May 1939.

12.2.2 Deportation lists

Some German towns have published lists of people deported from their town. It should however be borne in mind that some people may have been forced to move from their normal place of residence before being deported. Yad Vashem, Jerusalem, Israel, also holds some of these lists.

12.2.3 Memorial books

The German Government in 1986 issued *Gedenkbuch: Opfer der Verfolgung der deutschen Juden*, a memorial book in two volumes, which however only covered the former West Germany. The volumes include the names of about 125,000 'German' Jews. These were not limited by citizenship or birth but rather included all Jews resident in Germany who had been murdered. They are arranged in alphabetical order by surname, giving date of birth and so on. Where the place of death is not known the word '*Verschollen*' (missing) is written, indicating that the individual was deported but nothing further is known. *Für tot Erklärt* means declared dead by a German court. When newer sources of information and the former Eastern Germany are included it is expected that the number of names will rise to about 200,000. (Jews from other countries, such as Hungary or Poland, who were shipped to Germany for forced labour and then were murdered or died there were not included in the old Gedenkbuch and will not be included in the new one.)

Apart from the above, many towns and some states also have published their own memorial books. Amongst these are Berlin, Cologne (Köln), Frankfurt/Main, Fürth, Hamburg, Hanover, Leipzig and Nuremberg (Nürnberg). Books for other towns are constantly being prepared. They are too numerous to mention and many need updating, owing to new data continually becoming available.

While some of these books give only the name, date of birth and date and place of death (if known), others give details of the individuals, names of their parents, spouses and siblings and other information, some also including photographs. Several lists can be searched on the Internet, and some memorial books and other Holocaust-related material may be found at the Wiener Library.

Wiener Library, 4 Devonshire Street, London, W1W 5BH
Tel: 020 7636 7247   Fax: 020 7436 6428
E-mail: info@wienerlibrary.co.uk
Website: *www.wienerlibrary.co.uk*

The library collection has been built up over seventy years. The current holdings consist of around 60,000 books. The main focus, as would be expected, is on the fate of European Jews during the Third Reich and the history of the Third Reich in general. It also has Europe's foremost collection of books on the Holocaust. They also have many older books on European Jewish communities. In addition, the library has a very important photographic archive of around 10,000 images.

THE FOLLOWING LIBRARIES HAVE COLLECTIONS:

The British Library, Oriental & India Office Collections
96 Euston Road, London, NW1 2DB
Tel: 020 7412 7873 Fax: 020 7412 7641
Web: www.bl.uk/collections/orientalandindian.html
OIOC pages for family history researchers:
    www.bl.uk/collections/oiocfamilyhistory/family.html
Email: oioc-enquiries@bl.uk

Cambridge University Library
West Road, Cambridge, CB3 9DR
Tel: 01223 333000
E-mail: library@lib.cam.ac.uk
Website: www.lib.cam.ac.uk

The Jewish Genealogical Society of Great Britain
Library and Resource Centre, 33 Seymour Place, London, W1H 5AP
E-mail: library@jgsgb.org.uk
Website: www.jgsgb.org.uk

Leopold Muller Memorial Library
Oxford Centre for Hebrew & Jewish Studies, Yarnton Manor, Yarnton, Oxfordshire, OX5 1PY
Tel: 01865 377946 Fax: 01865 375079
E-mail: enquiries@ochjs.ac.uk
Website: www.ochjs.ac.uk (by appointment)

London School of Jewish Studies (formerly Jews' College)
Schaller House, 44a Albert Road, London, NW4 2SJ
Tel: 020 8203 6427 Fax: 020 8203 6420
Email: info@lsjs.ac.uk
Website: www.lsjs.ac.uk

Hartley Library
University of Southampton, Highfield, Southampton, SO17 1BJ
Tel: 023 8022 2180 Fax: 023 8022 3007
E-mail: libenqs@soton.ac.uk

School of Oriental & African Studies (SOAS)
University of London, Thornhaugh Street, Russell Square, London,
   WC1H OXG
Tel: 020 7637 2388 Fax: 020 7436 3844
Website: www.soas.ac.uk

University College, London
Gower Street, London, WC1E 6BT
Tel: 020 7679 2000
Website: www.ucl.ac.uk

Wiener Library (Institute of Contemporary History)
4 Devonshire Street, London, WIW 5BH
Tel: 020 7636 7247 Fax: 020 7436 6428
E-mail: info@wienerlibrary.co.uk
Website: www.wienerlibrary.co.uk

Yizkor books were written after the Holocaust as memorials to Jewish communities destroyed in the Holocaust. They were usually put together by survivors from those communities and contain descriptions and histories of the *shtetl* (small town/village/Jewish community), biographies of prominent people, lists of people who perished and other details. They are often embellished with photos, maps and other memorabilia.

Further reading
A list of *Yizkor* books, *shtetl* by *shtetl* alphabetically, has been compiled by Zachary Baker and can be found in Arthur Kurzweil's book *From Generation to Generation* (Harper-Perennial, 1994).

Cyril Fox and Saul Issroff, *Jewish Memorial (Yizkor) Books in the United Kingdom, Destroyed European Communities* (Jewish Genealogical Society of Great Britian, 2006).

12.3 Holocaust research

You will find a global list of Holocaust museums at *www.science.co.il/Holocaust-Museums.asp*. The primary sources for Holocaust research are listed below.

12.3.1 Yad Vashem Martyrs' and Heroes' Remembrance Authority

PO Box 3477, 91034 Jerusalem
Tel: +972 2 644 3400   Fax: +972 2 644 3443
E-mail: general.information@yadvashem.org.il
Website: *www.yadvashem.org*

Yad Vashem, Jerusalem, is the Jewish people's memorial to the murdered 6 million and symbolizes the ongoing confrontation with the rupture engendered by the Holocaust. The archive collection, the largest and most comprehensive repository of material on the Holocaust in the world, comprises 62 million pages of documents, nearly 267,500 photographs along with thousands of films and videotaped testimonies of survivors. These may be accessed by the public and read and viewed in the appropriate rooms. The library houses some 100,000 titles in many languages, thousands of periodicals and a large number of rare and precious items, establishing itself as the most significant Holocaust library in the world. The Hall of Names is a tribute to the victims by remembering them not as anonymous numbers but as individual human beings. The Pages of Testimony are symbolic gravestones, which record names and biographical data of millions of martyrs, as submitted by family members and friends. To date Yad Vashem has computerized 3.2 million names of Holocaust victims, compiled from approximately 2 million Pages of Testimony and various other lists.

12.3.2 United States Holocaust Memorial Museum

100 Raoul Wallenberg Place, SW Washington, DC 20024-2126
Tel: +1 202 488 0400 (general enquiries)
E-mail: archives@ushmm.org
Website: *www.ushmm.org*

The United States Holocaust Research Institute houses a Holocaust library and archive as well as photograph and oral history archives. It has records of most of the concentration camps, killing centres and ghettos. It also has the Registry of Jewish Holocaust Survivors, now known as the Names Registry.

12.3.3 Holocaust Education Trust

BCM Box 7892, London, WC1N 3XX
Tel: 020 7222 6822   Fax: 020 7233 0161
E-mail: info@het.org.uk
Website: *www.het.org.uk*

The Holocaust Educational Trust was established in 1988. Its aim is to educate young people from every ethnic background about the Holocaust and the important lessons to be learned for today. The Trust works in schools, universities and in the community to raise awareness and understanding of the Holocaust, providing teacher training, an outreach programme for schools, teaching aids and resource material.

12.3.4 The House of the Wannsee Conference

Am Grossen Wannsee 56-58, D-14109 Berlin
Tel: +49 30 80 50 01 0   Fax: +49 30 80 50 01 27
E-mail: library@ghwk.de
Website: *www.ghwk.de*

The Wannsee Villa contains an exhibition showing the entire process of the Holocaust, from segregation and persecution to the deportation and eventual murder of the Jews of Germany and all the lands conquered by the Third Reich. There is a very good library, with a wealth of material including registers with names, and written requests will be answered. An excellent and inexpensive booklet is available describing the exhibition.

12.3.5 International Tracing Service (ITS)

Große Allee 5–9, 34444 Bad Arolsen
Tel: +49 56 91 62 90   Fax: +49 56 91 62 95 01
E-mail: itsdoc@its-arolsen.org (documents) or
itstrace@its-arolsen.org (tracing section)
Website: *www.its-arolsen.org/english/index.html*

The ITS was set up at the end of the Second World War by the British Red Cross in Arolsen, Germany. It holds records of civilians who suffered in the Holocaust and details of concentration camps. Enquiries take a considerable time (see FAQs).

AUSCHWITZ
Most of the original death books were destroyed. Remaining death books from Auschwitz were published in three volumes in 1995 by Auschwitz Museum, POB 32-603, Oswiecim 5, Poland. Death books for Auschwitz Remnants Ed. J. Debski 1995.
Website: www.auschwitz.org.pl.
A limited number of records have been computerized by the United States Holocaust Memorial Museum. For details see: www.ushmm.org.
Auschwitz Jewish Centre see: *www.ajcf.org*.

BELZEC
Was originally set up as a forced labour camp but became a death camp in 1942, when 550,000 Jews were killed there between March and December of that year. There are no lists. Website: *www.belzec.org.pl*. Information in Polish only.

BERGEN BELSEN
Prisoners from all over Europe. A 'Gedenkbuch Haftlinge des Konzentrations-lager Bergen Belsen' (Memorial book of prisoners of the Concentration Camp Bergen Belsen) exists. Lists also include maiden name, date and place of birth and date of death, if known, but not religion. It also names many survivors who died some months after liberation. Address: Stiftung nieder-sachsische Gedenkstatten *(www.stiftung-ng.de)* Gedenkstatte Bergen-Belsen, D-29303 Lohheide, Germany.
E-mail: Bergen-Belsen@t-online.de.
Tel.: ++49 5051-4759-0 or ++49 5051-6011 Fax: ++49 5051-4759-18 or ++49 5051-7396 Website: *www.bergen-belsen.de*

BUCHENWALD
Buchenwald, in Thuringia, was one of the earlier concentration camps. The US National Archives has an extensive collection of records from this camp. Website: www.buchenwald.de. Data on 707 Hungarian Jewish survivors on Website: *www.jewishgen.org/databases/holocaust*

DACHAU
Dachau was the earliest major concentration camp. Two books have been published listing some of those who died there. The National Archives in College Park, Maryland, USA and in New York have film containing personnel records from Dachau. Also Dachau Foundation in Dachau has computerized all Dachau records and researchers may write to: Dachau KZ Gedenkstatte, Alte Romerstrasse 75, Dachau, Germany.
Tel: +49 8131 669970 Fax: +49 8131 2235 E-mail: info@kz-gedenkstaette-dachau.de. Website: *www.kz-gedenkstaette-dachau.de*

FLOSSENBÜRG, GERMANY, BAVARIA

Flossenbürg did not contain many prisoners until 1943. Between 1943 and 1945, however, nearly 97,000 persons, including about 10,000 Jews - mostly from Hungary, Czechoslovakia and Poland, were sent there and about 30,000 persons died in the camp or in the death marches, which took place near the end of the War. Information on 18,334 prisoners interned here.

Website: *www.jewishgen.org/databases/Holocaust*

GROSS-ROSEN, POLAND

In 1992 the Gross Rosen Museum issued Ksiega Zmarlych Wiezniow Kl, Gross Rosen. This book lists 8,887 names. Gross Rosen Museum and Archives 58-304 Walbrzych, Szarych Szeregow Street 9.

Tel: (0-74) 842-15-80 Tel/Fax (0-74) 842-15-94

E-mail: muzeum@gross-rosen.pl. Website: www.gross-rosen.pl

IZBICA

Thousands of German and Austrian Jews were sent to Izbica, which mainly acted as a collection camp. Most persons were then transferred to killing centres. There are no lists of people who died there or in the death camps of Chelmno, Sobibor or Treblinka.

LODZ

Records of the Lodz ghetto exist - 5 volumes were published under the title 'Lodz - Names'. Many may have lost their lives after the ghetto was liquidated in 1944 and inmates were sent to other camps.

RAVENSBRÜCK

Ravensbrück was primarily a concentration camp for women but it held about 20,000 men too. Prisoners came from all over Europe, with about 20 per cent from Germany, although most of the German prisoners seem to have been non-Jews. The US Holocaust Memorial Museum has four reels of film listing transport to and from Ravensbrück. Researchers may also write to: Mahn und Gedenkstaette Ravensbrück, Strasse der Nationen 1, D 16798 Fuerstenberg/Havel, Germany.

Tel: +49-33093-608-0   Fax: +49-33093-608-29

E-mail: info@ravensbrueck.de   Website: www.ravensbrueck.de

The records are in chronological order of transports with no index of names. It may therefore be difficult to find information.

SACHSENHAUSEN

Like Buchenwald, this camp, which was situated just north of Berlin, was used after Kristallnacht to hold German Jews, most of whom were later released. The Russians seized virtually all the records, and copies are kept in the US Holocaust Memorial Museum, Sachsenhausen Museum, Strafie der Nationen 22, D-16515 Oranienburg. Tel. +49-(0)3301-200-0

THERESIENSTADT (TEREZIN)
Theresienstadt had excellent records on all persons sent there, and those transferred to other camps. Virtually complete records are held at: Terezin Museum and Memorial, Pamatnik Terezin, 411 55 Terezin, Czech Republic.
Tel: +42-416-782-225, 782 442, 782 131 Fax: +42-416-782-245, 782 300
E-mail: archiv@pamatnik-terezin.cz.
Website: *www.jewishgen.org/bohmor/czechguide.html*
Also: Information about Jews deported to Ghetto Terezin, is available for a fee at: Beit Terezin Givat Haim Ihud, Mobile Poste Emek Hefer, 38935, Israel.
Tel: 04-6369515 or Fax: 04-6369793
E-mail: bterezin@ghi.org.il or visit the website at: *www.bterezin.org. il*
They hold in a card-index with all known details of about 160,000 prisoners who were in ghetto Terezin, and also of Jews under 'Protectorat', that were deported to the East before the ghetto was established in autumn 1941. The files include, for the most part, name, maiden name, date of birth, place, if further transported to another camp, transport number and whether they survived.

MINSK AND MALY, TROSTINEC
These were not concentration camps in the usual sense of the word. The Minsk ghetto had two parts. One part held largely local Jewish residents. In addition, about 35,000 Jews from Austria, Bohemia, Germany and Moravia were sent either to Minsk or Maly Trostinec. Most persons were murdered within a few days of arrival. There are virtually no victim lists for either Maly Trostinec or Minsk, other than the records relating to their transportation there. Very few survived.

12.3.6 Archive of Holocaust, Jewish Museum in Prague

U Stare Skoly 1, 110 00 Prague 1, Czech Republic
Tel: +420 221 711 511   Fax: +420 221 711 584
E-mail: office@jewishmuseum.cz
Website: *www.jewishmuseum.cz*

This is responsible for the administration of the Terezin Archive Collection, which contains official documents associated with the activities of the Jewish Council of Elders and their offices in the Terezin ghetto, the estates of Terezin prisoners (literary works, music scores, theatre plays, diaries, albums, magazines) and personal narratives of Holocaust survivors. The second archive collection, Persecution Documents, contains various archive documents and estates from the Holocaust period, which did not originate in the Terezin ghetto, and personal narratives concerning the period of Nazi persecution.

12.4 Further information

12.4.1 Stammbaum

www.jewishgen.org/stammbaum
This journal of German-Jewish genealogical research is the only genealogical source written in English that focuses exclusively on German-speaking Jewry. Published since 1992, it has attracted an international readership of professional and amateur genealogists, and facilitates the exchange of helpful and sound information, techniques, sources, and archival material. It includes human interest and anecdotal material, which add verisimilitude to genealogical data. While *Stammbaum* focuses on Germany, its scope also includes Austria, Switzerland, Alsace, Bohemia, and other areas with linguistic and historic relevance. A special feature entitled 'Mostly Holocaust: Sources & Resources' compiled by Peter Landé appears in volume 13 issued in May 1998.

12.4.2 Internet

The useful Internet site 'German/Austrian Holocaust-Related Databases on the Web' compiled by Peter Landé is at *www.jewishgen.org/GerSig/holocaust.htm.* This gives some short explanations about various databases and their Internet addresses where information on some of the memorial (*Yizkor*) books can be searched online. The JewishGen Holocaust database also contains 1.6 million entries about the Holocaust and survivors: see *www.jewishgen.org/databases/Holocaust.* You might also like to consult the book by Gary Mokotoff, *How to Document Victims and Locate Survivors of the Holocaust* (Avotaynu, 1995), which describes the major sources of information such as the Pages of Testimony, International Tracing Service and *Yizkor* books as well as sources unique to specific geographical localities. There is also a chapter on how to locate survivors. A major portion of the book is available on the Internet at *www.avotaynu.com/Holocaust.*

12.5 Museums

12.5.1 Imperial War Museum, Holocaust Exhibition

Lambeth Road, London, SE1 6HZ
Tel: 020 7416 5320   Fax: 020 7416 5374
E-mail: mail@iwm.org.uk
Website: *www.iwm.org.uk*

The Imperial War Museum's permanent Holocaust Exhibition uses historical material to tell the story of the Nazis' persecution of the Jews and other groups before and during the Second World War. The display covers two floors and brings to this country for the first time rare and important artefacts, some of them from former concentration and extermination camp museums in Germany, Poland and the Ukraine. These include photographs, documents, newspapers, posters and film, offering stark evidence of persecution, slaughter, collaboration and resistance. The exhibition is free.

12.5.2 The Holocaust Centre, Beth Shalom

Laxton, Newark, Notts. NG22 OPA
Tel: 01623 836627   Fax: 01623 836647
E-mail: office@bethshalom.com
Website: *www.bethshalom.com*

This is an important educational study centre, library and exhibition on the history of the Holocaust set up and built attached to their home by members of the Smith family. The centre, which has also published a number of books of Holocaust survivor testimonies, is not open to the general public, but only to pre-booked groups. To visit you should arrange to join a group. For further information contact the centre at the above address. There is also a mail-order book service for Holocaust publications and educational resources.

Note: the Imperial War Museum and Beth Shalom are not equipped to handle individual research enquiries.

12.6 Archives in Germany

Most town or state archives have documents relating to the Holocaust. What is available varies from place to place.

12.6.1 Stiftung Neue Synagoge Berlin – Centrum Judaicum

Oranienburger Strasse 28/30, D-10117 Berlin
Tel: +49 30 88 02 83 00   Fax: +49 30 88 02 84 83
Archives and Library: Tel: +49 30 88 02 84 25
Fax: +49 30 88 02 84 05
E-mail: Archive: archiv@cjudaicum.de
Library: bibliothek@cjudaicum.de
Website: *http://mysql.snafu.de/cjudaicum/index.html*

This holds many records of the former Reichsvereinigung der deutschen Juden, which include deportation lists as well as Heimeinkäufe für Theresienstadt, that is, legal documents detailing lists of assets and properties, which individuals had to 'sell' before their deportation.

12.7 Association of Jewish Refugees (AJR)

Jubilee House, Merrion Avenue, Stanmore, Middx. HA7 4RL
Tel: 020 8385 3070 Fax: 020 8385 3080
E-mail: enquiries@ajr.org.uk
Website: *www.ajr.org.uk*

The AJR provides an extensive range of social and welfare services, and grants financial assistance to Jewish victims of Nazi persecution living in Great Britain. Founded in 1941 by Jewish refugees from central Europe, the AJR has accumulated more than sixty years' experience attending to the needs of Holocaust refugees and survivors who came to this country before, during and after the Second World War. About 75,000 refugees, including approximately 10,000 children on the *Kindertransport* arrived in Britain from Nazi-occupied Europe in the late 1930s. New waves of immigration to Britain of former Nazi persecutees followed the 1956 Hungarian revolution, the 1967 Czech uprising and the break-up of the Soviet Union after 1989.

Today, membership is extended to all Jewish victims of Nazi persecution, their spouses, children and grandchildren, and the AJR counts as its members former refugees from all Nazi-occupied countries.

12.8 *Kindertransport* (Children's transport)

Kindertransport was the informal name of a rescue effort which brought thousands of refugee Jewish children to Great Britain from Nazi Germany between 1938 and 1940. The British Committee for the Jews of Germany, in cooperation with the Movement for the Care of Children from Germany, persuaded the British Government to permit an unspecified number of children under the age of 17 to enter Great Britain from Germany and German-occupied territories (Austria and the Czech lands). Private citizens or organizations had to guarantee to pay for each child's care, education and eventual emigration from Britain. In return for this guarantee, the British Government agreed to permit unaccompanied refugee children to enter the country on simple travel visas. Parents or guardians could not accompany the children.

Kindertransport statue at Liverpool Street Station designed by the renowned Israeli artist and former Kindertransport *refugee Frank Meisler.* (© Association of Jewish Refugees)

The first children's transport arrived in Harwich on 2 December 1938, bringing about 200 children from a Jewish orphanage in Berlin. The last transport from Germany left in September 1939. The last transport from the Netherlands left on 4 May 1940, the day that the country surrendered to Germany. Most of the transports left by train, leaving from Berlin, Vienna, Prague and other major cities in central Europe. The trains travelled to ports in Belgium and the Netherlands, from where the children sailed to Harwich.

Some of the children from Czechoslovakia were flown by plane directly to Britain. In all, the rescue operation brought about 9,000 to 10,000 children to Britain. Tragically, hundreds of children from the children's transports were trapped in Belgium and the Netherlands by the German invasion.

After the children's transports arrived in Harwich, those children with sponsors went to London to meet their foster families. Those children without sponsors were housed in a summer camp in Dovercourt Bay and in other facilities until individual families agreed to care for them or until hostels could be organized to care for larger groups of children. Jews, Quakers and Christians of many denominations worked together to bring refugee children to Britain.

In 1940, British authorities interned as enemy aliens about 1,000 children from the children's transport programme on the Isle of Man and in other internment camps in Canada and Australia. Despite their classification as enemy aliens, some of the boys from the *Kindertransport* joined the British Army and fought in the war against Germany.

After the war, many of the children became citizens of Great Britain, or emigrated to Israel, USA, Canada and Australia. Most of these children would never see their parents again as they had been murdered during the Holocaust.

זכור  Remember

Chapter 13

NAMES

This is a very complex subject with a tremendous amount written about it. Before the beginning of the early nineteenth century, Jews were known by their first names and their father's given name. For example, Baruch ben Yitzkak (Baruch 'son of' Yitzkak). In Eastern Europe, until the Napoleonic years of the early nineteenth century Jews did not get surnames. On arrival in the UK a number of families adopted the name of the town or city where they lived, while others took on the surname of their trade or had surnames assigned to them, often colours – for example, Hamburger (from Hamburg); Schneider (Tailor) or Goldstein (gold stone). After Napoleon's defeat many Jews dropped their surnames and returned to 'son of' names like Jacobson.

There were also forced names. A law was passed in the late eighteenth century by Joseph II of Austria that all Jews adopt a hereditary surname. In 1938/39 a law was passed in Nazi Germany forcing all Jews to register the additional Jewish first names of Israel for a man and Sara(h) for a woman as from 1 January 1939 and additional entries of these were made in the birth registers. For genealogical purposes these forced additional first names should be disregarded.

13.1 Jewish names

13.1.1 Tradition

Ashkenazi Jews traditionally named their children after deceased relatives, in order to honour the dead and to keep the dead person's memory alive. However, Sephardic Jews name them after living relatives. The firstborn son or daughter is usually named after the paternal grandfather or grandmother, the second son or daughter after the maternal grandfather or grandmother, the next children after their paternal or maternal uncle or aunt. Boys are normally named at their *B'rit Milah* ceremony and girls at a naming ceremony, usually held in a synagogue.

13.1.2 Why are Hebrew names required?

A number of Jewish religious ceremonies require Hebrew names. In the synagogue, Hebrew names are used for calling males over the age of 13 to the Torah. The memorial prayer and the prayer for the sick both include a person's Hebrew name. Legal documents such as the *Ketubah* or *Get* also include the Hebrew names.

13.1.3 Spelling and pronunciation

The spelling of names can cause problems when searching for surnames, whether Jewish or not. There can be so many variations, for example, Goldston, Goldstone and Goldstein. This is why it is essential to check all possible spellings especially when looking at the census. Another problem that arises is language variations. For example, German surnames beginning with 'W' were pronounced with a 'V' in England.

As with any other common surname, common Jewish surnames are difficult to find as there are so many people with the same name – Cohen, Levy and Greenberg for instance. Some people with the surname of Cohen changed their names to Conroy, Cohn or Kahn. Sometimes names were varied by making them plural, for example Solomon and Solomons or Isaac and Isaacs. You should also check on the spelling of first names – Laurence or Lawrence, Derrick or Derek – so that you have the correct version on your family tree.

13.1.4 Nicknames

It is very important to find out the correct name of a person, since it can be very misleading when a nickname supersedes the person's given name(s) on official documents. Nicknames are fine and can be shown on your family tree, but the correct full name *must* take priority. In addition, some people may use their middle name rather than their first name: this should be recorded and taken into account when researching the person concerned.

13.1.5 Change of name

As I have said above, a number of Jewish people changed their surnames. My parent's marriage certificate (shown on the following page) shows my father's surname as Molen (previously Vandermolen).

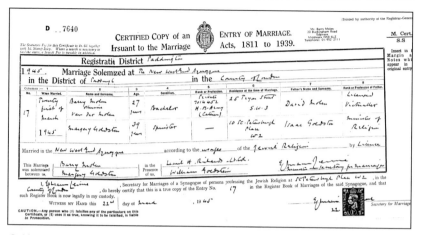

Goldston–Molen marriage certificate. This example shows the change of surname.

According to the National Archive's website, there are lots of legal ways to change a name. One way, the deed poll, gave the deed recording the name change to the person who changed their name. Where people paid extra to have this deed enrolled in court, the National Archives will have a copy. However, the majority of people did not enrol the deed in court. Most people who go to the National Archives looking for an enrolled change of name are disappointed. For further information see the National Archives website (*www.nationalarchives. gov.uk/catalogue/Leaflets/ri2250.htm*) and the UK Deed Poll Service website (*http://www.ukdps.co.uk/WhatIsADeedPoll.html*).

13.1.6 20,000+ Names from around the world!

http://www.20000-names.com/index.htm
This website has thousands of names from around the world sorted and categorized by country, language and meaning. Many of the names include detailed etymology; all include meaning. It includes both Hebrew and Yiddish names.

Further reading
Alexander Beider, *A Dictionary of Jewish Surnames from the Russian Empire* (Avotaynu Inc., 1993).

—, *A Dictionary of Jewish Surnames from the Kingdom of Poland* (Avotaynu Inc., 1996).

—, *A Dictionary of Jewish Surnames from Galicia* (Avotaynu Inc., 2004).

Chapter 14

MEDICAL

Have you ever thought about compiling your own family medical history? I guess this is rather a strange thing to write about, but, if you think carefully, it would provide information of the diseases and conditions that are common to your family and may help future generations in early prevention. Try to collect as much information as you can on as many generations as possible: this will give much better results in the long term. However, whether the information is obtained from death certificates or from family members, it must be accurate. The conditions in question could be cancer, stroke, heart disease, allergies, asthma, clinical depression, miscarriages, learning disabilities and so on. For example, muscular dystrophy is an hereditary disease passed down through male lines; Tay-Sachs disease is an inherited metabolic disorder and a well-documented Jewish genetic disease, potentially affecting one in every 2,500 Ashkenazi Jewish newborns. This is the kind of information that could be of great value to future generations. Having said this, in years to come, advances in genetic testing may be able to provide information on all the diseases you are at most risk from. When approaching your family, they may be loath to give you this information as illness is a very personal thing and they may not wish to discuss it or for others to know about it. If this is the case, it is important to accept their wishes, but you should explain to them why you want it and this may change their mind. Anything as personal as this should be treated confidentially. If this suggestion appeals to you, you may wish to look at the Mayo Clinic website (*www.mayoclinic.com/health/medical-history/HQ01707*) where you will find an article (HQ01707) on how to compile your family medical history.

14.1 Genetic diseases

14.1.1 Mazornet's Jewish diseases website

There are nearly 4,000 known genetic diseases that afflict the world's population. However, in almost every ethnic, racial, or demographic group, certain genetic diseases occur at higher frequencies among their members than in the general population. Such is the case for the Jewish people. The genetic diseases described on Mazornet's Jewish diseases website (*www.mazornet.com/genetics/ index.asp*) are disorders that occur more frequently in individuals of Jewish ancestry.

14.1.2 Genealogy by genetics

The JewishGen website (*www.jewishgen.org/dna*) also covers this subject under 'Genealogy by Genetics'.

14.2 Doctors in the family?

14.2.1 Where do I start?

The starting point for anyone with an ancestor who was a doctor is to refer to the following two publications: the *Medical Directory* is a commercial publication which contains information about most UK doctors. It gives fuller information than the *Medical Register* and includes details of Medical School attended, speciality, major published papers and previous posts. A full set back to the 1850s is kept in the Archives of the British Medical Association. Current editions may also be seen in the reference section of most libraries.

The *Medical Register* is a comprehensive list of UK doctors who have been accepted on the register. It does not, however, give much information. A full set back to the 1850s is kept in the Archives of the British Medical Association. The General Medical Council website (*www.gmc-uk.org*) includes the current database: select 'check a doctor's registration'.

14.2.2 Follow-up

In order to follow up on any information you may have acquired from the *Medical Directory*, it might be worthwhile making contact with your ancestor's Medical

School or the Royal College, as they too may keep records or be able to point you in the right direction (addresses on page 140).

14.2.3 Obituaries

Obituaries may appear in the *Lancet*, first published in 1823, and the *British Medical Journal* (known as the *BMJ*), first published in 1840. Bound volumes of these journals will be found in the Wellcome Library, Euston Road, London, which is open free to the public (*see 6.10 for further details*).

14.2.4 Qualifications

To check a doctor's qualifications, contact the General Medical Council (GMC) which holds information about all the doctors registered to practise in the UK on its List of Registered Medical Practitioners, which is updated daily. This register includes general information such as name, GMC reference number, dates of registration (provisional, full, specialist or limited), gender, current registration status, primary medical qualifications and specialist qualifications.

14.2.5 Checking historical records of the medical register

For those engaged in family history research, the GMC are able to search historical copies of the *Medical Register* published between 1859 and 1950. This is a free service for members of the public seeking biographical information about individual doctors. If you would like the GMC to do this for you, please contact the Information Access Team, providing as much detail as possible, for example, the doctor's name, date of birth and address. If you go to the GMC's website (*www.gmc-uk.org/register/search/index.asp*), the team's contact details and a request form can be found on the 'Freedom of Information' page. Please note: the GMC is unable to search historical copies of the *Medical Register* published after 1950. But most large public libraries will hold copies.

14.2.6 Inscriptions

When tracing your family history, always look out for every possible clue. The caduceus (serpent and staff) on the left of the following stained-glass window is the common symbol of the medical profession. This has presumably been incorporated into the design because the window was presented to the synagogue in memory of a doctor.

Note the serpent and staff, which represent the medical profession. (Reproduced with permission from St Albans United Synagogue)

14.2.7 Archaic medical terms

If you are stuck with a cause of death on a death certificate or other such docu-ment, the following websites will probably be of help to you. *www.paul_smith.doctors.org.uk/archaicmedicalterms.htm* is a very informative website which includes medical symbols, abbreviations and qualifications, archaic medical terminology found on old death certificates and much more. Several thousand more archaic medical terms (including German) can be found on *www.antiquus-morbus.com.*

14.2.8 Useful addresses

GENERAL MEDICAL COUNCIL (GMC)
Regent's Place, 350 Euston Road, London, NW1 3JN
Tel: 0845 357 3456
E-mail: gmc@gmc-uk.org
Website: *www.gmc-uk.org*
There are offices in Manchester, Edinburgh, Cardiff and Belfast.

BRITISH MEDICAL ASSOCIATION (HEAD OFFICE) (BMA)
BMA House, Tavistock Square, London, WC1H 9JP
Tel: 020 7387 4499 (general enquiries)   Fax: 020 7383 6400
E-mail: enquiries via the website feedback form
Website: *www.bma.org.uk*

ROYAL COLLEGE OF GENERAL PRACTITIONERS
14 Princes Gate, Hyde Park, London, SW7 1PU
Tel: 0845 456 4041   Fax: 020 7225 3047
E-mail: info@rcgp.org.uk
Website: *www.rcgp.org.uk/default.aspx?page=93*
MRCGP/FRCGP = Member/Fellow of the above College

ROYAL COLLEGE OF OBSTETRICIANS AND GYNAECOLOGISTS
27 Sussex Place, Regent's Park, London, NW1 4RG
Tel: 020 7772 6200   Fax: 020 7723 0575
E-mail: library@rcog.org.uk
Website: *www.rcog.org.uk*
MRCOG/FRCOG = Member/Fellow of the above College

ROYAL COLLEGE OF SURGEONS OF ENGLAND
35-43 Lincoln's Inn Fields, London, WC2A 3PE
Tel: 020 7405 3474
Library and archives: Tel: 020 7869 6555   Fax: 020 7405 4438
E-mail: library@rcseng.ac.uk
Website: *www.rcseng.ac.uk*
MRCS/FRCS = Member/Fellow of the above College

Chapter 15

HERALDRY

Jews have been using coats of arms as far back as the fourteenth century, not only privately but also in their official dealings with Gentiles, for example, in seals on legal documents. Stars of David, Jew's hats and menorahs that specifically refer to the Jewishness of the bearer – Jews used heraldry the same way others did. They used it in their homes, on their belongings, on their tombs; they used lions, eagles, ordinaries, and all sorts of charges. They also used canting devices and occasionally adopted or modified some famous Gentile family's coat, either as a mark of allegiance, or to claim a connection. Over time, Jews began to enter the ranks of the European nobility: as early as the seventeenth century the lion of Judah often takes the appearance of a heraldic lion rampant. The seal of Aaron of York, a prominent thirteenth-century English Jew, has not survived, but was said to display a human head. Jews were expelled in 1290 and do not reappear in England until the sixteenth century when Marranos, fleeing the Iberian peninsula, settled here. The first grant of arms to practising Jews was in 1723, for the Da Costa; Gules six broken shin-bones two, two and two barwise and the joints almost meeting each other in pale argent.

15.1 Well-known families

15.1.1 Sir Moses Montefiore

Sir Moses registered his arms in 1819 (argent a cedar-tree rising from rocks proper, on a chief azure a dagger erect proper pommel and hilt or of the first between two mullets of six points of the last), based on the family badge embroidered in an Ark curtain presented to the synagogue of Ancona by an ancestor in 1635. In 1831 he was allowed to add to the crest a banner inscribed with the word

Jerusalem in Hebrew, to commemorate a pilgrimage. In 1841, he was granted the privilege of supporters by Queen Victoria, although he was still only a knight bachelor. The supporters were a lion guardant and a stag proper, each supporting a flagstaff thereon hoisted a pennon forked with the word Jerusalem in Hebrew. He became a baronet in 1846 and died in 1885.

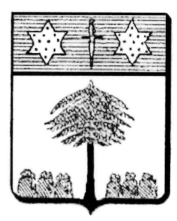

15.1.2 Rothschild

The name Rothschild comes from the red shield on the family's house in the Frankfurt ghetto; their name in the sixteenth century was N. Zum Roten Schild. When they moved out of the house they kept the name. In the eighteenth century, Amschel Rothschild founded the banking house. He had five

The coat of arms of Montefiore, London.

sons, Amschel, Salomon, Nathan, Carl and James, who founded branches in Vienna, London, Naples and Paris. They all provided great financial services to the enemies of Napoleon, and were consequently rewarded after Waterloo. The Austrian minister of finance, Count Stodion, proposed that they be ennobled as a way to get better interest rates on a loan. Metternich approved and, while the Frankfurt Jews still did not enjoy full civil rights, four of the brothers were granted German hereditary nobility (25 September and 21 October 1816). Nathan was not included because he was a foreign subject (in London).

The Rothschilds were asked to submit a coat of arms, which Salomon did: it consisted of quarterly 1) an eagle sable surcharged in dexter by a field gules, 2) gules a leopard passant proper, 3) a lion rampant, 4) azure, an arm bearing 5 arrows; in centre a shield of gules. The supporters were a greyhound and a stork, the crest a coronet with a lion issuant.

The Austrian Herald's College was very pernickety. They said that, as untitled nobility, the Rothschilds could have a helmet but not a coronet. The eagle alluded to Austria, the lion to Hesse-Kassel, and the leopard to England: the College said it was not in its power to use charges from other sovereign countries' arms. The five arrows

Coat of arms of the Rothschild family.

symbolized the five brothers: but since Nathan was excluded they could only have four arrows. The supporters were rejected, as well as the shield in the centre, as the privilege of the titled nobility. A patent for the modified arms was finally granted on 25 March 1817.

On 29 September 1822, the Austrian emperor made all five brothers hereditary barons. A revised coat of arms was registered, with the lion and the five arrows restored, and the escutcheon in centre, gules with oval target argent per bend sinister.

Nathan was authorized in 1838 to bear his Austrian title in England. His elder son Lionel was offered a British baronetcy in 1847, but he turned it down: it went to his brother Anthony. In 1885, the second baronet was made Baron Rothschild of Tring, the first Jew in the House of Peers.

15.1.3 Goldsmid

The first Jewish baronet was Isaac Lyon Goldsmid (title conferred 15 October 1841). He had received his title for his charitable work: he had been instrumental in the founding of University College, London. In 1846, he was made Baron de Goldsmid and de Palmeira in Portugal, and was authorized to use his titles in Great Britain the same year.

As noted above, in 1885 Sir Nathaniel Rothschild was the first Jewish peer. Later peers include Rufus Isaacs (Baron 1914, Viscount 1916, Marquis of Reading 1926), Samuel (Viscount Bearsted in 1925), Herbert Samuel (Viscount Samuel 1937), Montagu Samuel-Montagu (Baron Swaythling in 1907), Jessel (Baron Jessel in 1924). Their coats of arms sometimes contain allusions to their origins: the supporters of Lord Swaythling are 'soldiers of ancient Judea', the crest of Viscount Bearsted is 'a dexter arm embowed proper grasping a battle-axe argent, the head charged with two triangles interlaced sable' (i.e., the star of David).

Further reading
If you are interested in heraldry, you might like to consult AG Puttock's *A Dictionary of Heraldry and Related Subjects* (Blaketon Hall, 1985: ISBN: 0 907854 93 1). All the words above are explained in this dictionary.

There are also downloadable, electronic versions of Pimbley's *Dictionary of Heraldry* and *Symbolisms of Heraldry* on the website *FreeCoatsofArms.com*. For further information on heraldry, see *www.cyndislist.com/heraldry.htm*.

15.2 Institute of Heraldic and Genealogical Studies (IHGS)

79–82 Northgate, Canterbury, Kent, CT1 1BA
Tel: 01227 768664   Fax: 01227 765617
E-mail: ihgs@ihgs.ac.uk
Website: *www.ihgs.ac.uk*

Visitors wishing to use the library should make an appointment. They should not go with the express hope of discovering their ancestors in one place, but should be prepared to use the library as a step on their journey to discover what work has been done before, to localize possible origins and to examine the various indexes and guides available to assist them in their work. Researchers undertaking a one-name study will find the collections especially helpful.

15.3 The College of Arms

Queen Victoria Street, London, EC4V 4BT
Tel: 020 7248 2762   Fax: 020 7248 6448 (general enquiries)
Website: *www.college-of-arms.gov.uk*

The College of Arms is the official repository of the coats of arms and pedigrees of English, Welsh, Northern Irish and Commonwealth families. The College of Arms has no responsibility for Scotland and therefore is unable to answer any questions about clan membership, clan badges and so forth.

Note: there is no such thing as a 'coat of arms for a surname'. Coats of arms belong to individuals. For any person to have the right to a coat of arms they must either have had it granted to them or be descended in the legitimate male line from a person to whom arms were granted or confirmed in the past.

Beware: many firms and websites offer to produce coats of arms on a variety of merchandise bearing your 'personal crest' and charge considerable amounts for them.

15.4 Society of Genealogists (SOG)

For address and contact details *(see 6.8)*. The SOG publish a leaflet (No. 15) entitled 'The Right to Arms', which gives some basic information. Their website is *www.sog.org.uk/leaflets/arms.pdf*.

Chapter 16

UK CONNECTIONS

The following addresses may help to further your research. Where possible, I have included what the various organizations hold in the way of Jewish genealogical information.

16.1 Anglo-German Family History Society

20 Skylark Rise, Woolwell, Plymouth, Devon, PL6 7SN
Tel/Fax: 01752 310852
E-mail: jennytowey@blueyonder.co.uk
Website: *www.agfhs.org.uk*

The Anglo-German Family History Society welcomes all those who are interested in researching the genealogy or family history of people from the German-speaking parts of Europe who have emigrated over the centuries and settled in England, Scotland, Wales and Ireland (North and South), and the neighbouring islands.

16.2 Board of Deputies of British Jews (BOD)

6 Bloomsbury Square, London, WC1A 2LP
Tel: 020 7543 5400 (Central Enquiry Help Line)
Fax: 020 7543 0010
E-mail: info@bod.org.uk
Website: *www.bod.org.uk*

The Board was established in 1760 as a joint committee of the Sephardi and Ashkenazi communities in London. It plays a coordinating role in key issues affecting the Jewish community and promotes cooperation among different groups within the community. It conveys the views of the community to government and other public bodies on political and legislative matters that affect British Jewry.

16.3 East of London Family History Society (EoLFHS)

c/o 46 Brights Avenue, Rainham, Essex, RM13 9NW
Website: *www.eolfhs.org.uk*
The East of London Family History Society aims to promote and encourage the study of family history amongst those living in, or having ancestral links with, that area of Greater London north of the Thames extending from the edge of the City of London at Bishopsgate and Aldgate, eastwards through the London Boroughs of Hackney, Tower Hamlets, Newham, Redbridge, Barking and Dagenham, to the edge of Metropolitan Essex at Havering. The Society generally focuses on a variety of aspects of life in this area during the seventeenth, eighteenth, nineteenth and early twentieth centuries.

16.4 Federation of Family History Societies (FFHS)

PO Box 2425, Coventry, CV5 6YX
E-mail: info@ffhs.org.uk
Website: *www.ffhs.org.uk*
FFHS is an international organization, established in 1974 in the UK as a not-for-profit charitable company. It represents, advises and supports over 210 family history societies and other genealogical organizations worldwide, with a combined membership of over 300,000.

16.5 Friendly Societies

Dr Dan Weinbren, Chairman, Friendly Societies Research Group,
    Social Sciences, Gardiner Building, Open University,
    Walton Hall, Milton Keynes, MK7 6AA
Tel: 01908 654491
E-mail: d.weinbren@open.ac.uk
Website: *www.open.ac.uk/socialsciences/fsrg*
Friendly societies and mutual aid organizations were principally designed to help people protect themselves against problems which arose due to the illness or death of a breadwinner and have existed in the UK since at least the seventeenth century. Millions of people joined them in the nineteenth century and many societies still exist today. Although some restricted entry to local people, those in particular trades or Christians, Jews were members of many societies. For example, in East London there was a Jewish court (a branch) of one of the largest

societies, the Ancient Order of Foresters. There were also specifically Jewish friendly societies such as the Liverpool Chevra Toura, the Hebrah Kaddishah Meshivat Nefesh and the Jewish Brotherly Society, which was founded in 1823 and which probably merged into the United Jewish Hand-in-Hand Benevolent Society. There was at least one women's Jewish friendly society. Studies have been made of Jewish friendly societies in Manchester and London and Birmingham. The book *A History of the United Jewish Friendly Society 1949–1979* is kept at the library at Southampton University, as are some of that society's records and those of the societies which amalgamated to form it, the Order Achei Brith (founded 1888) and the Order Achei Ameth (founded 1897). Another source of information is graveyards, as Jewish friendly societies not only gave money to their members when they were sick or when sitting *shivah* (seven days of mourning) but also erected tombstones for them, often with the name of the society engraved upon the stone.

16.6 Hyde Park Family History Centre

Church of Jesus Christ of the Latter Day Saints (LDS/Mormons)
54-68 Exhibition Road, London, SW7 2PA
Tel: 020 7589 8561
E-mail: UK_LondonHydePark@LDSMail.net
Website: *www.hydeparkfhc.org/home.php*
The Church of Jesus Christ of the Latter Day Saints has a number of centres throughout the UK and across the world, all linked to the central genealogical library located in Salt Lake City, Utah *(see 17.23)*, where microfilms of the various indexes may be seen.

The Hyde Park Family History Centre is the largest of the centres in the UK. It has copies of the International Genealogical Index (IGI) and the library has over 2 million rolls of microfilmed records for practically every country in the world. A list of films of Jewish interest may be seen on the LDS website, which includes Jewish material from Poland, Lithuania, Austria and Hungary. (You do not have to be a member of this Church to use the genealogical research facilities.)

16.7 *Jewish Chronicle* (JC)

25 Furnival Street, London, EC4A 1JT
Tel: 020 7415 1500   Fax: 020 7405 9040
E-mail: jconline@chron.co.uk
Website: *www.thejc.com*
Since its foundation in 1841, the *Jewish Chronicle* (known as the JC) has carried obituaries for prominent members of the Jewish community. In some cases, the

inclusion of death notices or stone setting announcements may very well give the name of the cemetery, as well as other useful information about relatives. The *JC* is published weekly and sometimes the notice may not appear for a week or so after the person has died. In addition, note that there are two separate sections of births, marriages and deaths listed in each edition of the *JC* (a) Social & Personal (b) Classified. Back copies of the *JC* (1841 to the present) and other newspapers may be found at the British Library Newspaper Library.

THE *JEWISH CHRONICLE* ARCHIVES ONLINE
These are on the *Jewish Chronicle* website and date from the first edition in 1841 to the present. If you subscribe and receive your newspaper by post, you may gain access to this wealth of information. However, there is a charge if you require a copy of the particular page.

16.8 Jewish Historical Society of England (JHSE)

33 Seymour Place, London, W1H 6AP
Tel/Fax: 020 7723 5852
E-mail: info@jhse.org
Website: *www.jhse.org*

The society, the oldest historical and learned society of its kind in Europe, was founded in 1893 by the foremost Anglo-Jewish scholars and communal leaders of the day. Based in London, the society has active branches in Birmingham, Essex, Leeds, Liverpool and Manchester. It holds monthly meetings with lecturers on a wide range of subjects relating to Anglo-Jewish history.

The Anglo-Jewish Archives is an independent registered charity under the auspices of the JHSE. Genealogical collections have been deposited with the Society of Genealogists and the main archive collection has been deposited with the Hartley Library, University of Southampton.

16.9 Masonic records

Library and Museum of Freemasonry, The United Grand Lodge of
England, Freemasons' Hall, 60 Great Queen Street, London,
WC2B 5AZ
Tel: 020 7831 9811   Fax: 020 7831 6021
E-mail: libmus@ugle.org.uk (genealogical enquiries)
Website: *www.grandlodge-england.org*

The Library and Museum of Freemasonry houses one of the finest collections of Masonic material in the world. It is open to the public, Monday to Friday, free of charge. The Museum contains an extensive collection of objects with Masonic decoration including pottery and porcelain, glassware, silver, jewels and regalia. The Library and Archives are open for reference use. They contain a comprehensive collection of printed books and manuscripts on Freemasonry in England as well as material on Freemasonry elsewhere in the world and on subjects associated with Freemasonry or with mystical and esoteric traditions.

JEWISH FREEMASONRY

Originally it was not possible for Jews to be Freemasons, but from 1770 Jewish names appear in Lodge Lists, and a list of Jewish Freemasons in England in the eighteenth and early nineteenth centuries has been published in the *Transactions of the Jewish Historical Society*, vol. 25 (1977). In the nineteenth century there were a number of lodges that had a high proportion of Jewish members – Tranquillity, Joppa and the Lodge of Israel. In all, there must have been some thousands of Jewish masons in these few lodges, comprising mainly businessmen. All these lodges have produced their own respective histories, including details of members, often with name, address and trade. In addition, it is possible that if a person held office in the lodge there will be details in the history.

Further reading
George Rigal, 'Sources for Tracing Family History', *Shemot*, vol.1, no. 2 (Spring 1993).

16.10 National Archives Historical Manuscripts Commission (HMC)

The National Archives: Historical Manuscripts Commission Quality
House, Quality Court, Chancery Lane, London, WC2A 1HP
Tel: 020 7242 1198 Fax: 020 7831 3550
E-mail: nra@hmc.gov.uk
Website: *www.hmc.gov.uk*

In April 2003 the National Archives was launched, bringing together the Public Record Office and the Historical Manuscripts Commission. The National Archives now combines the services and expertise of both the former PRO and the HMC.

The National Register of Archives (NRA) contains information about the location and nature of historical records that have been created by some 46,000 individuals, 9,000 families, 29,000 businesses and 75,000 organizations. The NRA website is *www.nationalarchives.gov.uk/nra/default.htm*.

16.11 Royal Geographical Society (RGS)

Map Room, 1 Kensington Gore, London, SW7 2AR
Tel: 020 7591 3000   Fax: 020 7591 3001
E-mail: enquiries@rgs.org
Website: *www.rgs.org*

The Royal Geographical Society, together with the Institute of British Geographers, provides access to one of the world's largest and important geographical collections containing over 2 million maps, photographs, gazetteers, books, artwork, artefacts and documents. The collection tells the story of 500 years of geographical discovery and research.

It is essential to make an appointment to gain access to the collections. The Picture Library, Manuscript Archives and Expedition Report collection remain open to Fellows of the Society and to any member of the public whose requirements cannot readily be supplied through other resources.

16.12 School of Oriental and African Studies (SOAS) Library

University of London, Thornhaugh Street, Russell Square, London, WC1H 0XG
Tel: 020 7637 2388   Fax: 020 7436 3844
E-mail: libenquiry@soas.ac.uk
Website: *www.soas.ac.uk*

Comments received by email will receive a response within five working days. The library collects books, journals, electronic and multimedia items and has a Judaica collection.

Chapter 17

OVERSEAS CONNECTIONS

A s with the UK connections, the following overseas organizations hold a wealth of information relating to Jewish family history.

17.1 Australia

National Archives of Australia, Queen Victoria Terrace, Canberra

Postal address: PO Box 7425, Canberra, ACT 2610
Tel: +61 266 12 39 00   Fax: +61 262 12 39 99
Website: *www.naa.gov.au*

The registration of births, deaths and marriages in Australia was initially the responsibility of the colonies and, later, the states and territories. Enquiries about births, deaths and marriages within Australia should, in most cases, be directed to the registrar in the state or territory in which the event took place. To find out where registers for the Australian states and territories are held see fact sheet 89 on the above website.

Australian Jewish Historical Society

Level 2, Mandelbaum House, 385 Abercrombie Street, Darlington, NSW 2008
Website: *www.ajhs.info*

AJHS publishes the *Journal of the Australian Jewish Historical Society*, and maintains libraries and archives in Sydney and Melbourne. Its archives collect any material relating to history of Jewish settlement in Australia from 1788 to present day, and any material relevant to family history of present day descendants of Jewish settlers and convicts, such as

*   Great Synagogue: birth, deaths and marriages registers 1826–80s
*   community records: historical records 1840s–present day
*   synagogues: annual reports, 1840s–present day.

Australian Jewish Genealogical Society

Website: *www.ajgs.org.au/links.htm*

National Library of Australia

Canberra, ACT 2600
Tel: +61 262 62 11 11   Fax: +61 262 57 17 03
Website: *www.nla.gov.au/library*

The National Library of Australia is the country's largest reference library. Its role is to ensure that documentary resources of national significance relating to Australia and the Australian people, as well as significant non-Australian library materials, are collected, preserved and made accessible either through the library itself or through collaborative arrangements with other libraries and information providers. See the website catalogue for Jewish holdings.

TRACING YOUR FAMILY HISTORY IN AUSTRALIA

The following websites have extremely useful links for Australian genealogy in general:

> *www.coraweb.com.au/index.htm*
> *www.cyndislist.com/austnz.htm* (Jewish section).

17.2 Austria

Austrian Jewish Museum

A-7000 Iron City, Unterbergstrasse 6, P.O. Box 67
Tel: +43 026 82 65 14 55   Fax: +43 026 82 65 14 54
E-Mail: info@ojm.at
Website: *www.ojm.at*

The Austrian Jewish Museum was able to establish itself in a historical building of the former Jew lane of Iron City. It is thus at a place where for more than 250 years a considerable Jewish municipality has been settled. The museum was created in 1972 as the first Jewish museum in Austria after 1945.

Austrian National Library

Department for Reference and Information Services, Josefsplatz 1, A-1015 Vienna
E-mail: *awi@onb.ac.at*
Website: *www.onb.ac.at*

In the Austrian National Library (Österreichische Nationalbibliothek) you can view a number of useful resources. The entrance is from the Heldenplatz in front of the Hofburg palace, opposite the Volksgarten. The library has a newspaper archive downstairs, where you can view old copies of the *Neues Wiener Abendblatt* (microfilm 394.205 - D.Per) and the *Neue Freie Presse* (microfilm 393.929 - D). These are the two papers in which Jewish families always put death notices. (The *Neue Freie Presse* runs from 1885–January 1939. It is available at the British Library – Newspaper Library – *see 6.3.*) The notices usually contain names of all family members (also parents, brothers, sisters, in-laws, and so forth). You can also consult there *Lehmann's Wiener Wohnungsanzeiger* (cat. 393.867 - C.Per). This is an alphabetical listing of all heads of household in Vienna from 1859 onwards. It is like a telephone directory for the nineteenth century without telephone numbers. The Mormon FHL has these directories available for 1870, 1902, 1906, 1908 and 1925.

Jewish Museum Archives

Dorotheergasse 11, A-1010, Vienna
Tel: +43 15 35 04 31 / ext. 212
E-Mail: archiv@jmw.at
Website: *www.jmw.at*

This archive contains valuable seventeenth-century marriage contracts as well as the 1941 diary of a young Viennese Jew. These graphic artworks, photographs, documents and manuscripts are fragmentary snapshots of Jewish life. The archive is open to visitors by prior appointment.

Jewish Museum Library

Seitenstettengasse 4, 1010 Vienna
Tel: +43 1 5 35 04 31 / ext. 410   Fax: + 43 15 35 50 46
E-mail: bibliothek@jmw.at
Website: *www.jmw.at*

The reference library contains approximately 41,000 works from the last four centuries in German, Hebrew, Yiddish and English. The main focus lies in the history of the Jews in Austria and of the Jewish community of Vienna. The library also houses an important collection of rabbinical works and other religious writings.

17.3 Belarus

National Archives of the Republic of Belarus

43 Kirova Street, 220030, Minsk, Republic of Belarus
Tel: +375 172 22 32 29   Fax: +375 172 22 32 85
E-mail: narb@infonet.by
Website: *http://archives.gov.by/eng*
The Belarusian archives hold a large number of documents which are used in genealogical research and can be of interest to those who are researching their family history (parish registers, census records, military records, records of various institutions, religious communities, social groups, nationalities, etc.). Most are held in the National Historical Archive of Belarus in Minsk (the former Minsk, Mogilev and Vitebsk provinces and a part of the Grodno province of the Russian Empire) and the National Historical Archive of Belarus in Grodno (the former Grodno and Vilno provinces). Information on genealogy can also be found in the state archives for registration of vital statistics ZAGS.

17.4 Belgium

Jewish Museum of Belgium

Av. de Stalingrad, Brussels
Tel: +32 (0)2 51 21 963
Website: *www.mjb-mjb.org*
The collections of the Jewish Museum of Belgium chiefly depict the life and history of the Jewish populations of the regions, starting in the eighteenth century.

TRACING YOUR FAMILY HISTORY IN BELGIUM
The following websites have useful links for Belgian genealogy in general: *www.cyndislist.com/belgium.htm* and *http://surf.to/BEL-archives.*

17.5 Canada

Library and Archives Canada

395 Wellington Street, Ottawa, ON, K1A ON4
Tel: + 1 613 9965115
Website: *www.collectionscanada.ca*
Library and Archives Canada collects and preserves Canada's documentary heritage, and makes it accessible to all Canadians. This heritage includes publications, archival records, sound and audio-visual materials, photographs, artworks, and electronic documents such as websites. As part of their mandate, they work closely with other archives and libraries to acquire and share these materials as widely as possible.

Ottawa Jewish Archives

21 Nadolny Sachs Private, Ottawa, ON, K2A 1R9
Tel: + 1 613 7984696 / ext. 260   Fax: + 1 613 7984695
E-mail: archives@jewishottawa.com
Website: *www.ottawajewisharchives.ca*
The Ottawa Jewish Archives is dedicated to the objectives of gathering, recording and preserving the collective memory of the Jewish community of Ottawa, and of making the holdings of historical records, memorabilia, and artefacts accessible to all persons for their use, well-being and enjoyment.

Jewish Heritage Centre of Western Canada

Suite C116, 123 Doncaster Street, Winnipeg, MB, R3N 2B2
Tel: +1 204 4777460   Fax: +1 204 4777465
E-mail: heritage@jhcwc.org
Website: *www.jhcwc.org*
Included in the collection of material pertaining to the Jewish People of Western Canada are about 5,000 photographs, many rare and unique; 500 taped interviews with summary transcripts; archival documents totalling over 300 linear feet of shelf space; hundreds of books on local Jewish history, including many on

genealogy and many on the Holocaust; collections of family trees and histories; vertical files of clippings and miscellaneous materials; back issues of local Jewish newspapers to the 1910s and a computerized index of the articles from them; photographs of almost all the cemetery stones from all the Jewish cemeteries in Manitoba; an amazing and wonderful collection of artefacts and objects from our past; and much more.

THE JEWISH HERITAGE CENTRE OF WESTERN CANADA'S COMPUTER DATABASE
This database includes over 14,000 news stories and over 29,000 articles. The articles are of most interest to genealogists, as they include over 18,000 references to articles with the category 'genealogy'. They are made up of mostly birth announcements, bar mitzvahs, engagements, weddings, obituaries, memorials, and other social announcements. In most cases, all the relatives mentioned in the article are listed in the database.

17.6 Czech Republic

Jewish Museum and Library in Prague (JMP)

U Stare Skoly 1, 110 00 Prague 1
Tel: +420 221 711511   Fax: +420 221 711584
E-mail: office@jewishmuseum.cz
Website: *www.jewishmuseum.cz*
The current JMP library contains as many as 100,000 volumes, including Hebrew books stemming mainly from the territory of Bohemia and Moravia, as well as other areas of Europe. The library contains literature dealing with Jewish history in Bohemia and Moravia and, last but not least, a large collection of Judaica on various topics (history, history of art, philosophy, bibliography, linguistics, fiction). The JMP library also has a large and valuable collection of periodicals comprising historical items (newspapers, revues and year-books from the nineteenth and first half of the twentieth centuries) as well as recent and contemporary titles which the library purchases or exchanges with other Czech and foreign institutions. See Chapter 12 on the Holocaust for further details of the museum's holdings.

Czech State Archives

Statni Istredni Archiv, tr. Milady Horakove 133,
CZ-166 21 Praha 6
Tel: +420 974 847825   Fax: +420 233 320274
E-mail: na1@nacr.cz
The archive holds the vital records of the former Jewish communities of Bohemia and Moravia. Unfortunately, the records are in German and difficult to read.

Federation of the Jewish Communities of the Czech Republic

Maiselova 18, CZ-110 01 Praha 1
Tel: +420 223 18559   Fax: +420 223 16728
The Federation is responsible for and maintains most of the Jewish cemeteries and synagogues in the Czech Republic.

TRACING YOUR FAMILY HISTORY IN THE CZECH REPUBLIC AND SLOVAKIA
The following websites have useful links for Czech genealogy in general: *www.cyndislist.com/czech.htm* and *www.jewishgen.org/bohmor/czechguide.html*.

17.7 Denmark

Danish National Archives

Rigsdagsgarden 9, DK 1218 København
Tel: +45 3392 3310   Fax: +45 3315 3239
Website: *www.sa.dk*
There are a few pieces of information which are very important in your search for Danish ancestors. In particular, knowledge of the four points mentioned below is vital:

1. The birthplace of one or several relatives in Denmark (parish or town), year and, if possible, the date.
2. The date of emigration.
3. The last permanent address in Denmark.
4. The Danish version of the family name at the time of the emigration.

If you are fortunate enough to be in possession of a birth certificate or a marriage certificate, service records or other documents issued by the Danish authorities, you are well on your way, but also letters from family in Denmark may be of great help. Postmarks, where the letter is sent from or the return address, can also be sources that may give an important clue, and sometimes a photograph from Denmark may give valuable information.

Danish Jewish Museum (Dansk Jødisk Museum)

Det Kongelige Biblioteks have, Proviantpassagen 6, DK 1218 København
Tel: +45 3311 2218   Fax: +45 3311 2290
E-mail: info@jewmus.dk
Website: *www.jewmus.dk*

The Danish Jewish Museum collects and preserves all material which can document significant aspects of Jewish life in Denmark. The collection includes, among other things, paintings, drawings, prints, photographs, silverware, textiles, books, newspapers, scrapbooks, postcards, theatre programmes, memoirs, letters, films, videos, audio recordings and records.

TRACING YOUR FAMILY HISTORY IN DENMARK
The website *www.cyndislist.com/denmark.htm* gives useful links for Danish genealogy in general.

17.8 France

Etsi, Sephardi Genealogical and Historical Review Society

E-mail: laurphil@wanadoo.fr
Website: *www.geocities.com/EnchantedForest/1321*

Etsi (Hebrew for '*my tree*') is the first Sephardi Genealogical and Historical Society, founded in 1998 in Paris. The purpose of *Etsi* is to help people interested in Jewish genealogical and historical research in the Sephardi world. *Etsi*'s field of study covers the Ottoman Empire (Turkey, Greece, Palestine, Syria, Libya, Egypt), North Africa (Algeria, Morocco, Tunisia), Spain, Portugal, Italy and Gibraltar.

TRACING YOUR FAMILY HISTORY IN FRANCE
The website *www.cyndislist.com/france.htm* has useful links for French genealogy in general.

17.9 Germany

Landesarchiv Berlin

Kalckreuthstrasse 1-2, D-10777, Berlin
Tel: +49 (0)30 212 830
E-mail: info@landesarchiv-berlin.de
Website: *www.landesarchiv-berlin.de*

The archive holds lists of Berlin deportations, including documentation of seizure of assets, and information relating to the Jewish community of Berlin.

State Archive Stuttgart

Konrad-Adenauerstrasse 4, D-780137 Stuttgart
Email: Hauptstaatarchiv@s.lad-bw.de
Website: *www.lad-bw.de*

All search facilities in this archive are based on German content and databases.

Jewish Museum Berlin

Lindenstraße 9-14, 10969, Berlin
Tel: +49 (0)30 259 93 300   Fax: +49 (0)30 259 93 409
E-mail: info@jmberlin.de
Website: *www.juedisches-museum-berlin.de*

Approximately 700 collections of documents, photos and mementos of individual and family histories are collected and catalogued in this historical archive. Particularly impressive are the legacies relating to the fates of families during the era of Nazi persecution, including documents on emigration and life in exile, last messages from victims of the Holocaust and correspondence with the *Wiedergutmachungs* (recompensation) authorities after 1945. Oral and written documents supplement the archive collection. They offer additional means of understanding Jewish life in Germany.

The Leo Baeck Institute in New York has recently opened a research branch in Germany at the Jewish Museum Berlin. Researchers in Berlin may use all the LBI archives microfilms and the photograph database. Anyone wishing to visit the LBI, Berlin, must first contact the archivist there, Mr Aubrey Pomerance, on *a.pomerance@jmberlin.de*. See also Leo Baeck Institute (German Jewry), 17.23.

Central Archives for Research on the History of the Jews in Germany

Zentralarchiv, Bienenstr. 5, 69117 Heidelberg
Tel: +49 (0)62 211 64141   Fax: +49 (0)62 211 81049
E-mail: Zentralarchiv@urz.uni-heidelberg.de
Website: *http://www.uni-heidelberg.de/institute/sonst/aj/englisch.htm*

The Central Archives for Research on the History of the Jews in Germany was founded in 1987 as an establishment of the Central Council of Jews in Germany (Zentralrat der Juden in Deutschland). The concept of the Central Archives can be compared with that of the former General Archives of the German Jews (*Gesamtarchiv der deutschen Juden*) located in Berlin (1905–39). Storing and cataloguing historically valuable documents from Jewish communities, associations, organizations, and persons are of major concern. As a rule, the records are deposited at the Central Archives.

Collections

CEMETERY DOCUMENTATION
Nearly 2,000 Jewish cemeteries exist today in the Federal Republic of Germany. The total number of Jewish gravestones has been estimated at 600,000. Photographs of about 54,000 Jewish tombstones in Baden-Württemberg are now in possession of the Central Archives. In addition, the Central Archives stores photographs of more than 5,000 Jewish gravestones from Lower Saxony.

NEWSLETTERS
The collections of the Central Archives consist of public newspapers and journals, newsletters of Jewish communities, programmes of Jewish adult education centres, and photocopied circulars.

LIBRARY
The library of the Central Archives is a reference library. In order to acquire the fonds (record groups) and collections of the Central Archives, the library not only offers general reference books but also publications on the Jewish history in post-war Germany and Jewish regional history.

TRACING YOUR FAMILY HISTORY IN GERMANY
The website *www.cyndislist.com/germany.htm* has useful links for German genealogy in general.

17.10 The Netherlands (Holland)

Jewish Historical Museum

Jonas Daniel Meijerplein 2-4, (Nieuwe Amstelstraat 1), Amsterdam
Postal address: PO Box 1673, 1001 RE Amsterdam
Website: *www.jhm.nl*

The Museum is the only museum in the Netherlands to focus on Jewish history, religion and culture. The museum is located in a group of four historical Ashkenazi synagogues at the heart of the former Jewish quarter in the centre of Amsterdam.

Netherlands Society for Jewish Genealogy

Nederlandse Kring voor Joodse Genealogie, PO Box 94703, 1090 GS Amsterdam
E-mail: info@nljewgen.org
Website: *www.nljewgen.org*

Increasing interest in genealogy during recent decades resulted in 1987 in the formation of the Netherlands Society for Jewish Genealogy. In the fifteen years of its existence it has grown to a membership of more than 750.

Historisch onderzoeksbureau Dutch Archives

t.a.v. dhr. E. Ruijssenaars, Hoflaan 10, NL-2321 TB, Leiden
Tel: +31 (0)71 5727 381
E-mail: info@dutcharchives.com
Website: *www.dutcharchives.com*

These Dutch archives specialize in genealogical and other historical research in archives and libraries, answering questions like 'Where did somebody live?', 'Where did someone work?', 'What did the house or business look like?', 'What happened on a certain date?'. Translations are provided on request.

TRACING YOUR FAMILY HISTORY IN THE NETHERLANDS

The website *www.cyndislist.com/nether.htm* has useful links for Dutch genealogy in general. In addition, there is the Dutch Jewish Genealogical Database – 'Ashkenazi Amsterdam in the Eighteenth Century' on *http://tinyurl.com/2xa3u2*.

17.11 Hungary

National Archives of Hungary

2-4 Becsi kapu Square, H-1014 Budapest
Postal address: PO Box 3, H-1250 Budapest
Tel: +36 1 225 2800   Fax: +36 1 225 2817
E-mail: info@mol.gov.hu
Website: *www.mol.gov.hu*

Jewish Museum and Archives of Hungary

Dohany u. 2, H-1077, Budapest
Tel: +36 1 342 8949
E-mail: bpjewmus@visio.c3.hu
Website:
www.fsz.bme.hu/hungary/budapest/bpmuz/bpmuz19.htm

Budapest City Archives (Stadtarchiv Budapest)

Teve u. 3-5, H-1139 Budapest
Tel: +36 1 298 7500
E-mail: bfl@bparchiv.hu
Website: *www.bparchiv.hu/demo/angol/angol.html*

17.12 India

Council of Indian Jewry

c/o The Jewish Club, Jerro Bldg., second floor, 137 Mahatma
Gandhi Road, Bombay 400 023
Tel: +91 22 270461 or +91 22 271628

USEFUL WEBSITES
www.haruth.com/AsianIndia.html (Jewish India)
www.kosherdelight.com/Indiasynagogues.htm (synagogues)
http://adaniel.tripod.com/beneisrael.htm (Jews in India)

17.13 Israel

Central Archives for the History of the Jewish People

46 Jabotinsky Street, Jerusalem
Postal address: POB 1149, Jerusalem 91010
E-mail: archives@vms.huji.ac.il
Website: *http://sites.huji.ac.il/archives*

The Central Archives began in 1938 as the Jewish Historical General Archives. They were re-established by the government of Israel in 1969 as the Central Archives for the History of the Jewish People, with one of its major aims being to compile a central catalogue of comprehensive material about the Diaspora, a great part of which was hitherto unknown, and to enable historians and scholars to avail themselves of the data thus gathered. Its focus is worldwide, and it has strong collections on French, Italian, German and Austrian Jewry. Only scattered records from Eastern Europe.

Israel Genealogical Society

PO Box 4270, Jerusalem 91041
Tel: +972 8 6880884
Website: *www.isragen.org.il*

The Israel Genealogical Society is Israel's premier genealogical organization. Founded in 1983, the IGS is a not-for-profit organization with branches in Jerusalem, Tel Aviv, Netanya, the Negev, Beit Shemesh and Haifa. As a service to those researching their roots in Israel the society has uploaded Israel Pickholtz's article 'New Limitations from the Ministry of Internal Affairs on Access to Israeli Documents', published in the February issue of their journal *Sharsheret Hadorot* (vol. 21, no.1). The article, in English and Hebrew, can be found at *www.isragen.org.il/NROS/BIB/SHD/selected.html*.

Israel State Archives

35 Makor Hayim Street, Jerusalem 91919
Tel: +972 2 588 3986
Postal address: Israel State Archives, Prime Minister's Office,
Qiryat Ben-Gurion, Bldg. 3, Jerusalem 91919
Tel: +972 2 5680612, +972 2 5680680   Fax: +972 2 5680670
E-mail: star_pmo@mail.gov.il (general)
E-mail: michals@int.gov.il (research)
Website: *www.isragen.org.il/ROS/ARCHIVES/archive-state-2.html*

Closed on Fridays, Saturdays, Jewish holidays and the last two weeks of August. Appointments recommended. The Israel State Archives were founded in 1949, one year after the establishment of the State of Israel, to safeguard the records of the preceeding governmental administrations of Palestine from the Ottoman Period to the end of the British Mandate, and to document the development of Israel.

Jewish National and University Library

**Hebrew University of Jerusalem, Edmond Safra Campus,
Givat-Ram, Jerusalem 91004
Tel: +972 2 658 5027
Website: *www.huji.ac.il***

(Also incorporates the International Institute for Jewish Genealogy)
The *Ketubot* digitization project aims to create a worldwide registry of *Ketubot* in public and private collections throughout the world. Based on the collection of the Jewish National and University Library with over 1,200 items, the project contains *Ketubot* originating from dozens of different countries, and covering a time period of over 900 years. It is a major resource for research in Jewish history, law and art.

Yad Vashem Martyrs' and Heroes' Remembrance Authority *(see also 12.3.1)*

**PO Box 3477, Jerusalem 91034
Tel: +972 2 644 3400   Fax: +972 2 644 3443
E-mail: archive@yad-vashem.org.il
Website: *www.yadvashem.org***

17.14 Italy

Genealogy of the Jews in Italy

**E-mail: info@italian-family-history.com
Website: *www.italian-family-history.com***

TRACING YOUR FAMILY HISTORY IN ITALY
The website *www.cyndislist.com/italy.htm* has useful links for Italian genealogy in general.

17.15 Latvia

Latvian State Historical Archives

Slokas iela 16, Riga LV-1048
Tel: +371 7 614008   Fax: +371 7 612406
E-mail: irinwein@latnet.lv

The Latvian State Historical Archives holds vital records (births, marriages and deaths) from 1854, the year they started to be held officially, up to 1905. There are some years beyond these dates. Among other records held is the first all-Russian census of 1897. Records for 1906–21 are held at the Archives of the Registry Department, Kalku Street 24, Riga LV-1050, Latvia. For a complete inventory of Jewish holdings in the Latvian State Historical Archives, see the Shtetlinks Riga website (*www.shtetlinks.jewishgen.org/riga/rigapage.htm*).

Jewish Museum

6 Skolas Street, Riga LV-1322

The museum has recently been renovated and has many moving exhibits and photos. Visitors are welcome and a short video is shown depicting the tragedy of the Holocaust in Latvia. The Jewish Community Centre is on the ground floor in the same building as the museum.

TRACING YOUR FAMILY HISTORY IN THE BALTIC STATES
The website *www.cyndislist.com/baltic.htm* has useful links for Latvian genealogy in general.

Further reading
Arlene Beare, *Jewish Ancestors: A Guide to Jewish Genealogy in Latvia and Estonia* (2006: available from *www.jgsgb.org.uk*).

17.16 Lithuania

Lithuanian State Historical Archives

Gerosios Vilties 10, Vilnius LT-03134
Tel: +370 5 213 74 82   Fax: +370 5 213 76 12
E-mail: istorijos.archyvas@lvia.lt
Website: *www.archyvai.lt* (select language)

This archive contains pre-1940 vital records, some revision lists (census records), and various other types of records including a small number of pre-1914 internal passport records. All the Jewish vital records (over 500,000) were filmed by the Mormons except for those vital records transferred from Archive (B) in January, 2002. Some of these transferred records date back to 1881.

Kaunas Regional Archives

Maironio g. 28a, LT-44249 Kaunas
E-mail: archyvas@turbodsl.lt

The Regional Archives in Kaunas were founded in 1921 to collect and preserve the records of the agencies of state and local administration which functioned in the territory of Lithuania in the nineteenth/beginning of the twentieth centuries. Today, the Archives are one of the largest in Lithuania and preserve more than 1,200,000 files (12,000 shelf-metres) organized into 2,320 fonds (record groups). This archive contains pre-1915 records such as revision lists, various types of tax records, guild records, court records, and others. All these records were for cities and towns formerly located in the Kovno Gubernia region, which at one time covered the largest part of Lithuania.

Lithuanian Central Civil Register Archives

Kalinausko 21, 2600, Vilnius

This archive contains post-1940 vital records.

Vilna Gaon Jewish State Museum

Pylimo g. 4, LT-01117, Vilnius
Tel: +370 5 2127912   Fax: +370 52611946
E-mail: jewishmuseum@jmuseum.lt
Website: *www.jmuseum.lt*

The three main parts of the museum's collection include items from the pre-Second World War Vilnius museum, items from the pre-war historic ethnographic Kaunas Museum (both preserved by various Lithuanian museums), and items acquired by the contemporary museum since its inception. The collection includes ritual objects and everyday items used or produced by Lithuanian Jews; Jewish documentation such as books, letters, posters, cigarette packet pieces with handwritten notes, some copies of Ghetto diaries, seals of various organizations, translations, periodicals, proclamations and archival material from the former USSR.

TRACING YOUR FAMILY HISTORY IN THE BALTIC STATES
The website *www.cyndislist.com/baltic.htm* has useful links for Lithuanian genealogy in general. For frequently asked questions, see *www.jewishgen.org/LITVAK/faqs.htm*.

Further reading
Sam Aaron, *Jewish Ancestors: A Guide to Jewish Genealogy in Lithuania* (2005: available from *www.jgsgb.org.uk*).

17.17 New Zealand

New Zealand Jewish Archives

80 Webb Street, Wellington
Tel: +64 4 384 5081   Fax: +64 4 478 9061
E-mail: nzjewisharchives@ihug.co.nz
Website: *www.nzjewisharchives.org*
Since 1980 the New Zealand Jewish Archives has been collecting, storing, and filing documents, photographs, memorabilia, Judaica, books, pamphlets, newspaper cuttings, oral recordings and video tapes about Jewish life in New Zealand. The collection includes some of the earliest synagogue and other communal records for New Zealand. The archives are stored in several rooms within the Jewish Community Centre. There is no display area.

TRACING YOUR FAMILY HISTORY IN NEW ZEALAND
The websites *www.coraweb.com.au/nzsites.htm* and *www.cyndislist.com/newzealand.htm* have very little mention of Jewish genealogy but do have useful links for New Zealand genealogy in general.

17.18 Poland

Naczelna Dyrekcja Archiwow Panstwowych (Polish State Archives)

6 Dluga Street, 00-950 Warszawa, PO Box 1005
Fax: +48 22 635 6822
E-mail: ndap@archiwa.gov.pl
Website: *www.archiwa.gov.pl*

Records over 100 years old are located throughout a dozen or more regional archives, but write to the main archives listed above. Records less than 100 years old are still stored at the local Civil Registrar's office. According to JewishGen, Jewish vital records are held in seventy-five different branches of the Polish State Archives (PSA), located throughout Poland. For a table showing which archives branch holds the Jewish vital records for each town see *www.jewishgen.org/ infofiles/Poland/PolishTownsArchives.htm*.

Galicia Jewish Museum

Dajwor Street 18, 31-052 Krakow
Tel: +48 12 421 6842
E-mail: info@galiciajewishmuseum.org
Website: *www.galiciajewishmuseum.org*
Within this specially renovated and designed post-industrial building of 920 square metres, there is a large exhibition area and a café that can seat forty people. The museum has a bookshop concentrating on Jewish life and culture, with books in Polish, English and German, and on the Holocaust, Jewish thought, identity and literature. There is a small museum shop and a lecture room, which holds sixty people.

Lodz Synagogue *(see 5.1.7)*

TRACING YOUR FAMILY HISTORY IN POLAND
The websites *www.cyndislist.com/poland.htm* and *www.JewishGen.org./jri-pl* have useful links for Polish genealogy in general.

Further reading
Susan Fifer, *Jewish Ancestors: A Guide to Jewish Genealogy in Poland* (2007; available from *www.jgsgb.org.uk*).

17.19 Romania

Archivelor Statului din Republica Romania

Bdul Kogalniceanu nr. 29; Buceresti, Sect. 5
The archive is reportedly not responsive to mail requests; however, some on-site visits have been successful.

17.20 Slovakia

Statny Ustredny Archiv

Cesta 42, Bratislava
Jewish Vital Statistics Holdings in the Archives of Slovakia are available in microfiche from Avotaynu (*www.avotaynu.com*). The archive has a list of 4,000 towns, showing the location and scope of holdings of Jewish birth, marriage and death records.

17.21 South Africa

The National Archives of South Africa

24 Hamilton Street, Arcadia, Pretoria
Postal address: Private Bag X236, Pretoria 0001
Tel: +27 (0)12 323 5300   Fax: +27 (0)12 323 5287
Fax to e-mail: 086 682 5055
E-mail: Archives@dac.gov.za
Website: *www.national.archives.gov.za*
Each of the repositories which houses archival groups that contain genealogical information has prepared guides to genealogical research which enable the researcher or user to find the information required. The guides are fundamental to any genealogical research because they contain information that is specific to the sources for genealogical research for that particular repository and geo-political region. Some genealogical sources date back to the seventeenth century. You can order the guides from the National Archives Repository, the Pietermaritzburg Archives Repository, the Cape Town Archives Repository as well as the Free State Archives Repository by contacting these repositories at the addresses provided under contact information on the above website.

Tracing your family history in South Africa
The website *www.cyndislist.com/soafrica.htm* has useful links for South African genealogy in general.

17.22 Ukraine

Central State Historical Archives of the Ukraine, Kiev

ul. Solomenskaya 24, 252061 Kyiv
Tel: +380 44 277 3002

Most of the records from Eastern Galicia are in Warsaw and now coming online on the Internet.

17.23 USA

American Family Immigration History Center, Ellis Island

The Statue of Liberty-Ellis Island Foundation, Inc.
Attention: History Center, 292 Madison Ave, New York, NY 10017-7769
Tel: +1 212 561 4588
E-mail: historycenter@ellisisland.org
Website: *www.ellisisland.org*

The above centre, on Ellis Island was opened in 2001.

ELLIS ISLAND ARCHIVES

More than 22 million passengers and members of ships' crews entered the United States through Ellis Island and the Port of New York between 1892 and 1924. Information about each person was written down in ships' passenger lists, known as manifests. Manifests were used to examine immigrants upon arrival in the United States. You can now search free of charge these millions of records for information on individual Ellis Island passengers.

American Jewish Archives (American Jewry)

3101 Clifton Avenue, Cincinnati, OH 45220
Tel: +1 513 221 1875   Fax: +1 513 221 7812
Website: *www.americanjewisharchives.org/aja*

These Archives were founded in 1947 in the aftermath of the Second World War and the Holocaust. For over a half century, the American Jewish Archives have been preserving American Jewish history and imparting it to the next generation. The Jacob Rader Marcus Center of the American Jewish Archives, located on the Cincinnati Campus of Hebrew Union College-Jewish Institute of Religion, houses over 10 million pages of documentation. It contains nearly 8,000 linear feet of archives, manuscripts, photographs, audio and video tapes, microfilm, and genealogical materials.

American Jewish Historical Society

15 West 16th Street, New York, NY 10011
Tel: +1 212 294 6160   Fax: +1 212 294 6161
or 160 Herrick Road, Newton Centre, MA 02459
Tel: +1 617 559 8880   Fax: +1 617 559 8881
E-mail: info@ajhs.cjh.org
Website: www.ajhs.org

Founded in 1892, the mission of the American Jewish Historical Society is to foster awareness and appreciation of the American Jewish heritage and to serve as a national scholarly resource for research through the collection, preservation and dissemination of materials relating to American Jewish history. The American Jewish Historical Society is the oldest national ethnic historical organization in the United States. The society's library, archives, photograph, and art and artefacts collections document the American Jewish experience.

Center for Jewish History

15 West 16th Street, between 5th and 6th Avenues, New York, NY 10011
Tel: +1 212 294 8301

The Center for Jewish History is the home of five Jewish institutions dedicated to history, culture, and art. It unites under one roof collections that bring together centuries of Jewish life: The American Jewish Historical Society; The American Sephardi Federation; The Leo Baeck Institute; Yeshiva University Museum and the YIVO Institute for Jewish Research.

THE ACKMAN AND ZIFF FAMILY GENEALOGY INSTITUTE
Open 9.30 a.m.–5 p.m., Monday – Thursday

Federation of East European Family History Societies

PO Box 510898, Salt Lake City, UT 84151-0898
E-mail: info@feefhs.org
Website: www.feefhs.org

The Federation of East European Family History Societies (FEEFHS) was organized in 1992 and promotes family research in Eastern and central Europe without any ethnic, religious, or social distinctions. It provides a forum for individuals and organizations focused on a single country or group of people to exchange information and be updated on developments in the field. While it primarily serves the interests of North Americans in tracing their lineages back to a European homeland, it welcomes members from all countries.

The online map room's website is *www.feefhs.org/maps/indexmap.html*.

Leo Baeck Institute, New York (German Jewry)

15 West 16th Street, New York, NY 10011
Tel: +1 212 744 6400   Fax: +1 212 988 1305
E-mail: lbigenealogy@lbi.cjh.org
Website: *www.lbi.org*

The Leo Baeck Institute is devoted to studying the history of German-speaking Jewry from its origins to its tragic destruction by the Nazis and to preserving its culture. Dating back almost 2,000 years, when Jews first settled along the Rhine, the Jewish communities of Germany, Austria, and other German-speaking areas of Europe had a history marked by individual as well as collective accomplishments in communal organization and welfare, commerce, industry and politics, the arts and sciences, and in literature, philosophy and theology. The collections include many kinds of materials of use to genealogical researchers, including family trees, family histories, memoirs and Jewish community histories. All geographic areas where German was spoken are included in the scope of the collections.

The Church of Jesus Christ of the Latter-Day Saints (Mormons)

35 North West Temple Street, Salt Lake City, UT 84150-3400
Tel: +1 801 240 2584   Fax: +1 801 240 1794
E-mail: fhl@familysearch.org
Website: *www.familysearch.org*

Founded in 1894 to gather genealogical records and assist members of the Church of Jesus Christ of Latter-day Saints with their family history and genealogical research. It is the largest library of its kind in the world. Open to the general public at no charge. The website has information on Jewish research.

RECORDS COLLECTION:
The collection includes over 2.4 million rolls of microfilmed genealogical records; 742,000 microfiche; 310,000 books, serials, and other formats; 4,500

periodicals; 700 electronic resources. The Ancestral File database contains more than 36 million names that are linked into families. The International Genealogical Index database contains approximately 600 million names of deceased individuals. An addendum to the International Genealogical Index contains an additional 125 million names. These names have been patron submitted or extracted from thousands of original birth, christening and marriage records. The Pedigree Resource File database contains over 80 million names that are linked into families. Records available are from the United States, Canada, the British Isles, Europe, Latin America, Asia, and Africa.

THE KNOWLES COLLECTION

Website: *http://tinyurl.com/2wzjh2*
This collection contains information for thousands of Jews from the British Isles. Building on the work of the late Isobel Mordy, the collection links individuals into family groups.

YIVO Institute for Jewish Research

15 West 16th Street, New York, NY 10011
Tel: +1 212 246 6080
Website: *www.yivoinstitute.org*
Founded in 1925 in Vilna, Poland (now Vilnius, Lithuania), as the Yiddish Scientific Institute, the YIVO Institute for Jewish Research is dedicated to the history and culture of Ashkenazi Jewry and to its influence in the Americas. Headquartered in New York City since 1940, today YIVO is the world's preeminent resource centre for East European Jewish Studies, Yiddish language, literature and folklore and the American Jewish immigrant experience. The YIVO Library holds over 360,000 volumes in twelve major languages, and the archives contain more than 23,000,000 pieces, including manuscripts, documents, photographs, sound recordings, art works, films, posters, sheet music, and other artefacts.

Additional Resources

TRACING YOUR FAMILY HISTORY IN THE USA

The website *www.cyndislist.com/usa.htm* has useful links for American genealogy in general.

THE INTERNATIONAL ASSOCIATION OF JEWISH GENEALOGICAL SOCIETIES (IAJGS)

The IAJGS represents over eighty societies worldwide and lists can be obtained from its website (*www.iajgs.org*).

GLOBAL LIST OF JEWISH MUSEUMS

Website: *www.science.co.il/Jewish-Museums.asp*

GLOBAL LIST OF HOLOCAUST MUSEUMS

Website: *www.science.co.il/Holocaust-Museums.asp*

SOCIAL SECURITY DEATH INDEX (SSDI, USA)

Website: *http://ssdi.rootsweb.com*

The SSDI does not include the names of everyone, even if they had a Social Security Number (SNN). If relatives or the funeral home did not report the death to the Social Security Administration, or if the individual died before 1962 (when the records were computerized) then they probably will not appear in this database. The omission of an individual in this index does not indicate the person is still living. It simply means that there was no report of the person's death to Social Security Administration.

Chapter 18

CASE STUDIES

The three short case studies in this chapter are presented as a practical demonstration of how the information and clues provided by the range of documents I acquired from various archives and newspaper cuttings can be used in researching one's ancestry, and how it is possible even with those limited resources to trace one's roots back.

When I began researching my family history in 1984 I had only a small family tree, on paper rolled up in a drawer. In those days there were no computerized databases and the only way to obtain information from archival documents was by writing to the various archives. Today access to information is much easier, but the manner in which the material is used remains the same.

18.1 Where do I start?

Let me give three examples of how one finds family one has never heard of before from the smallest amount of information available and how one clue leads to another.

18.1.1 Barnett-Wolfers

Tracing Elizabeth Barnett (born 23 July 1858), daughter of Joshua and Nancy Barnett (née Benjamin, died 20 May 1898), was quite a remarkable piece of detective work! In an announcement of the death of her mother in the *Jewish Chronicle* in 1898, her children were listed. Unfortunately, the list gave only the married surnames of the female children, without any initials. Luckily, I knew who some of her sisters had married, which helped. However, the announcement left me with two unidentified married daughters, Mrs White and Mrs Wolfers. Now, I

Jewish Chronicle
Friday 27 May 1898
Death Announcement
BARNETT. On Friday, the 20 May, 104A Bridge Street, Burdett
Road, NANCY, relict of the late JOSHUA BARNETT, of 9
Harrow Alley, in her 75th year; mother of Baron Barnett, 12½
Artillery Passage, E.C., Elias Barnett, 26 Cutler Street, City; Mrs
White, 5 Tenter Street North; Mrs Taylor, 120 Antil Road, Bow;
Mrs Wolfers, 104D, Bridge Street; Mark Barnett, 60 Landseer Road,
N; Mrs Benabo, 17 White Horse Street, Bow; Abraham Barnett and
Mrs J Simmonds, 12 Ormside Street, S.E.
Deeply mourned by her loving children, sisters, grandchildren,
relatives and a large circle of friends.
May her dear soul rest in peace. Amen.
Foreign papers please copy

Extract from the Jewish Chronicle, *27 May 1898.*

knew that my great-uncle, Reverend Joseph Goldston, had been the Minister at
Swansea Synagogue. From an old *Jewish Year Book* I knew that a Reverend
Philip Wolfers had also been Minister at Swansea Synagogue and I wondered
whether the two families had known each other, which may have led to a marriage
between their children.

I therefore wrote to Swansea Synagogue to ask
them whether they could tell me the name of
Reverend Philip Wolfers' wife and whether he had
any family. They wrote back with a few details and
told me that he had moved on to Cardiff. Cardiff
Synagogue was extremely helpful and put me in
touch with the synagogue's archivist, who called the
next day to say that he had taken the liberty of
putting the details onto the Internet and he had
received three replies. It turned out that Reverend
Philip Wolfers had a brother, David, who had
married Elizabeth Barnett in 1882 and they
had eleven children between 1883 and 1903. Once
again, I had not only found some new deceased

*Elizabeth Barnett, b.1858,
d.1932.*

relatives but I also found details of their children plus, most importantly, one living relative, Estelle Wolfers.

Other options

Since the above announcement was dated 1898, I decided to have a look at the 1901 census. I found the Simmonds family and Abraham Barnett, now living at 106 Upper North Street, with a list of children which I did not have before. Mark Barnett was at the same address with a wife and children. Mr and Mrs Taylor were living alone also at the same address.

Now that I had this information, I checked in the *Jewish Chronicle* Archives to see if any of the new family members were listed. Luckily, there were numerous entries. I also checked the GRO index of births, marriages and deaths and recorded the information onto my database against each person. It is really important to check every possible lead when you find new relatives, and so exciting when you find new information.

Nehemiah Goldston, wearing the uniform of a Jewish chaplain in the First World War.

18.1.2 Goldston

My next example is rather a sad one. My great-uncle, Reverend Nehemiah Goldston (b. 2 December 1866), was the Minister of the South-East London Synagogue from its opening in 1889 and Hebrew Master at Westminster Jews' Free School. This was all I knew about him, apart from his being married to a lady called Floretta. Knowing that most of our family are buried at Willesden (United Synagogue) Cemetery, I contacted the cemetery office to ask if they could give me a list of people buried there with the surname of Goldston. They were extremely helpful and let me look at the records, which revealed quite a number of people with the name of Goldston of whom I had never heard. One was Ernest Goldston. I found his grave, and discovered that he was the child of Nehemiah Goldston.

What to do next

As I then knew his date of death, I visited the British Library Newspaper Library in Colindale and found his obituary in the *Jewish Chronicle*, which said that Nehemiah had two other sons. This was exciting new information. I put this news onto the Jewish Genealogical Society of Great Britain's (JGSGB) discussion group, asking for information about Nehemiah, whose tombstone, although in a very poor condition, had said he was Honorary Chaplain to the Forces in the First World War. The next day I received a reply from one of the JGSGB members, who told me that there was a photograph of Nehemiah in uniform in the *British Jewry Book of Honour*, together with a photograph of his son Lionel (I did not know about this son). I then visited the JGSGB library to look at the book and sure enough there were two superb photographs. Nehemiah was photographed with other chaplains and there was a photograph of Rifleman Lionel Emanuel Goldston 2130, 21st Battalion, London Regiment (1st Surrey Rifles).

With this information in hand, I then looked on the website of the Commonwealth War Graves Commission (*www.cwgc.org*) and found that he was killed in France on 30 May 1915 aged 19 and was buried in the Guards Cemetery, Windy Corner, Cuinchy, Pas de Calais, France. As we were going to Belgium for our holidays that year, my husband and I decided to visit the grave. The Commonwealth War Graves Commission (CWGC) keeps the graves in immaculate condition and we found Lionel's without any trouble. I felt rather sad and humble that eighty-four years had passed by, his parents had died years ago and I was now standing by a very brave young man's grave, which probably had not been visited for well over fifty years and may not be visited ever again. As is the Jewish custom when visiting a grave, we placed a stone on the grave.

18.1.3 Goldston-Sandelson

I knew that my grandfather (Reverend Isaac Goldston AKC) had a sister Frances (born 24 November 1875) but I knew absolutely nothing about her. At the British Library Newspaper Library in Colindale I came across an obituary of Reverend Nehemiah Goldston, which included the name of a Mrs Y M Sandelson of Newcastle. I was not sure who this was so I decided to write, on the off-chance, to the editor of the *North East Jewish Recorder*, asking for help.

To my astonishment, I received a couple of replies telling me that it was Frances who was the second wife of Rabbi Yochiel Mayer Sandelson, the Rabbi of Villa Place Beth Hamidrash in 1895, which then joined up with the Corporation Street Synagogue in 1925 and finally the Ravensworth Terrace Synagogue, which closed in 1970. Because they married late in life, there were no children. I was told that Frances had died in the North East Joel Intract

The Jacob Franklin Prize, awarded in 1888 for proficiency and good conduct.

Memorial Home in Sunderland. I, therefore, wrote to the home, and they confirmed this.

Another person replied and asked if I would like a Bible that had been presented to Frances as a prize. He also sent me a photograph of her.

This information was gathered about six to seven years ago. However, it is important when researching your family to look back every so often at the information you have been given to see whether any further information has come to light or whether you have missed any vital clues. Very recently, I wanted to find out where Frances was buried. None of our immediate family seemed to know. So, once again, I put details onto the JGSGB discussion group and sure enough I received a message back from a member living in Newcastle to say they knew where she was buried. To cut a long story short, I now have a photograph of her grave and also a photograph of Rabbi Sandelson's first wife's grave.

To reiterate what I have said in an earlier chapter, joining the Jewish Genealogical Society of Great Britain brings numerous advantages when tracing your family, as you will see from the response I received above.

GLOSSARY

Aliyah   Called up in synagogue to the reading of the
                                Law.

Ashkenazi (pl. Ashkenazim)   Descendants of Jews who lived in north-west
                                Europe (France, Germany and Holland) and
                                in Eastern Europe (Lithuania, Poland,
                                Russia and the Ukraine) until around 1900.

Bar Mitzvah   Following his 13th birthday, a boy is called
                                up in the synagogue to read a portion of the
                                Law.

Bat Mitzvah   A girl becomes Bat Mitzvah at the age of 12.

Beth Din   Rabbinical court.

B'rit Milah   Ceremony of circumcision which is carried
                                out on the eighth day of birth, unless there is
                                a medical problem (Genesis 17).

Chuppah   Canopy. Bride and Bridegroom stand
                                together under the *chuppah* during the
                                wedding ceremony.

Cohanim (pl. for Cohen)   Direct descendants of Moses' brother Aaron,
                                the first priest; historically Cohanim served
                                as the Temple priests.

Get   Divorce.

Halachically   According to Jewish law and customs.

Ketubah (pl. *Ketubot*)   Marriage contract.

Kosher   All food permitted in Jewish law is
                                described as being kosher, or fit for use.

Levi	Descendants of Jacob's son Levi and his tribe; historically, Levites served as assistants to the Temple priests.
Magen David	Shield/Star of David.
Marrano	Families who were ostensibly Christian but who secretly practised Judaism.
Mikveh (pl. *Mikvot*)	Ritual bath.
Minyan	A quorum of ten or more adult Jewish males (over the age of 13) required for a communal religious service.
Mishnah	Learning. The Oral Law was written down about 200 ce and put into its present order by Rabbi Judah Hanasi.
Pesach	Passover.
Sefer Torah	*Pentateuch (the first five books of the Old Testament).*
Sephardi	Sephardic Jews lived in Spain until the fifteenth century. After the expulsion of Jews at this time, they travelled to Italy, North Africa, Turkey and back to the Middle East. In the early part of the sixteenth century, the Jewish immigrants who had settled in Italy were once again forced to leave and took up refuge in England. Some of these were musicians at the court of Henry VIII. Roger Prior, 'Jewish Musicians at the Tudor Court', *Musical Quarterly*, vol. 69, no. 2 (Spring 1983), pp. 253–65.
Shabbat	Sabbath (Friday sunset to Saturday sunset).
Shavuot	Pentecost.
Shivah	Seven. Seven days of mourning after the burial during which the mourners remain in their homes.

Shtetl (pl. *shtetlach*)   Little city, town or village. Often used to refer to the small Jewish communities of Eastern Europe where the culture of the Ashkenazim flourished before the Second World War.

Stille chuppah   Silent marriage.

Tallit   Prayer shawl.

Talmud   A sacred book containing the interpretations of the Jewish laws which are found in the Bible.

Yahrzeit   Anniversary of a death.

Yeshiva (pl. *Yeshivot*)   Jewish institution for Torah study and study of the Talmud.

Yishuv   Settlement; referring to the Jewish community in Palestine prior to the declaration of the State of Israel.

Yisrael   Refers to a Jew who is neither a Levi nor a Cohen.

Yizkor   Prayer in remembrance of departed parents. Recited four times a year in the synagogue (with a minyan), at Yom Kippur, Shemini Atzeret, 8th day of Passover and 2nd day of Shavuot.

Yizkor books   These were written after the Holocaust as memorials to Jewish communities destroyed in the Holocaust.

BIBLIOGRAPHY

Abbreviations

Where given in bold, the following abbreviations indicate where a book may be located.

BL   British Library
JC   Jews' College Library (London School of Jewish Studies)
JGSGB Library of the Jewish Genealogical Society Great Britain
UCL   Jewish Studies Library, University College London
WL   Wiener Library, London

General

Cox, J, *Tracing Your Ancestors in the Public Record Office*, 4th edn (London, HMSO, 1990). **JGSGB**
Joseph, A, *My Ancestors were Jewish*, 3rd edn of Isobel Mordy's book, shown below (JGSGB, 2002).
Mordy, I, *My Ancestors were Jewish. How Can I Find Out More about Them?* (Society of Genealogists, 1995). **JGSGB**

There are also many useful articles in the Transactions of the Jewish Historical Society of England (JHSE – Transactions). A complete set (minus vol. 3) and index are available from the JGSGB Library.

Directories

Hartfield, G, *Commercial Directory of Jews in UK* (1984). **JC**
The Jewish Directory (1874). **JGSGB**
The Jewish Calendar, 1876, 1877, 1881, 1888, 1889, 1890 and 1896. **JC**

Towers, Regions and Jews

Newman, A, *Provincial Jewry in Victorian Britain* (The Jewish Historical Society, 1975). **JGSGB, UCL**

ABERDEEN
Weisman, M, 'The Aberdeen Hebrew Congregation', *Menorah*, vol. 3, no. 1 (1976).

BIRMINGHAM
Josephs, Z, *Birmingham Jewry 1749–1914* (The Birmingham Jewish Historical Research Group, 1980). **BL**
——, *Birmingham Jewry: More Aspects, 1740–1930* (The Birmingham Jewish Historical Research Group, 1984). **BL**
——, *Survivors: Jewish Refugees in Birmingham, 1933–1945* (Meridian Books, 1988). **UCL**

BRADFORD
Harris, S, 'A History of the Jewish Community in Bradford between 1870–1970', University of Sheffield PhD thesis, 1992.

BRIGHTON
Spector, D, 'The Jews of Brighton 1770–1900', *JHSE – Transactions*, 22 (1968–69).

BRISTOL
Samuel, J, *The Jews in Bristol: A History of the Jewish Community in Bristol from the Middle Ages to the Present Day* (Redcliffe Publications, 1997). **BL, JGSGB**
Tobias, A *et al*, *A Catalogue of the Burials in the Jewish Cemeteries of Bristol*. **JGSGB**

CANTERBURY
'Births, Marriages and Deaths of the Canterbury Congregation 1830–1869'. **The Hyamson Collection, JGSGB Library**
Cohn-Sherbok, D *et al*, 'The Jewish Community of Canterbury', *Kent Life*, November 1978, pp. 42–3.
Williamson, S, 'The Jewish Community of Canterbury', *Bygone Kent*, vol. 4, no. 3 (1983), pp. 174–6.

CARDIFF

Henriques, U Q, *The Jews of South Wales* (University of Wales Press, 1993), ch.1, 'The Jewish community of Cardiff, 1813–1914', pp. 9–44. **UCL**

——, 'The Jewish Community of Cardiff, 1813-1914', *Welsh History Review*, 14 (1988), pp. 269–300. **UCL**

CHATHAM

Green, G L, *The Royal Navy and Anglo-Jewry 1740-1820* (1989).

Jolles, M, *The Chatham Hebrew Society Synagogue Ledger 1836–1865* (privately printed, 2000).

CHELTENHAM

Torode, B, *Hebrew Community of Cheltenham, Gloucester & Stroud* (privately printed, 1999). **JGSGB**

COLCHESTER

Roth, C, 'An Eighteenth-Century Jewish Community in Colchester', *AJA Quarterly*, vol. 3, no. 2 (1957), pp. 22–5.

Weisman, M, 'Colchester and District Jewish Community', *Menorah*, vol. 16, no. 2 (1967), pp. 20–3.

CORNWALL

Pearce, K, and Fry, H, *The Lost Jews of Cornwall* (Redcliffe 2000). **JGSGB**

COVENTRY

Levine, H, *The Jews of Coventry* (1970).

DARLINGTON

Olsover L, *The Jewish Communities of North-East England 1755–1980* (Ashley Mark Publishing, 1980). **BL**

DEVON

Fry, H, *The Jews in North Devon during the Second World War* (Halsgrove, Tiverton, 2005).

EDINBURGH

Phillips, A, *A History of the Origins of the First Jewish Community in Scotland – Edinburgh, 1816* (John Donald, 1979). **BL**

FALMOUTH

Jacobs, A, 'The Jews of Falmouth', *JHSE –Transactions*, 17 (1951–2).

GATESHEAD

Levy, A, *Story of Gateshead Yeshiva* (Wessex Press, 1952).

Olsover, L, *Jewish Communities of North-East England 1755–1980* (Ashley Mark Publishing, 1980). **UCL**

GLASGOW

Collins, K E, *Be Well: Jewish Immigrant Health and Welfare in Glasgow 1860–1914* (Tuckwell Press, 2002).

——, *Glasgow Jewry: A Guide to the History and Community of the Jews in Glasgow* (Scottish Jewish Archives Committee, 1993). **JGSGB**

——, *Second City Jewry: The Jews of Glasgow in the Age of Expansion, 1790–1919* (Scottish Jewish Archives, 1990). **JGSGB**

——, *Go and Learn: The International Story of Jews and Medicine in Scotland 1739–1945* (Aberdeen University Press, 1988).

——, *Scotland's Jews: A Guide to the History and Community of the Jews in Scotland* (Scottish Jewish Archives Centre, 1999).

——, *Aspects of Scottish Jewry* (Glasgow Jewish Representative Council, 1987).

Cory, K B, *Tracing Your Scottish Ancestry* (Polygon, 1990).

Hutt, C A, and Kaplan, H, *Scottish Shtetl: Jewish Life in the Gorbals 1880–1974* (Gorbals Fair Society, 1984).

James, A, *Scottish Roots: A Step by Step Guide for Ancestor Hunters* (Pelican, 1982).

Levy, A, *The Origins of Glasgow Jewry, 1812–1895* (privately printed, 1949). **UCL**

——, *Origins of Scottish Jewry* (Jewish Historical Society of England, 1958).

Phillips, A, *A History of the Origins of the First Jewish Community in Scotland* (1st edn 1816; repr. John Donald, 1979).

Sinclair, C, *Tracing Your Scottish Ancestors: A Guide to Ancestry Research in the Scottish Record Office* (HMSO, 1990).

GLOUCESTER

Torode, B, *The Hebrew Community of Cheltenham, Gloucester and Stroud* (privately printed, 1999). **JGSGB**

GRIMSBY

Berman, J, 'Grimsby Hebrew Community Records', *Shemot*, vol. 8, no.2 (2000).

Gerlis, D and Gerlis, L, *The Story of the Grimsby Jewish Community* (Humberside Leisure Services, 1986). **UCL, JGSGB**

Grimsby Burial Board Register 1896–1995. **JGSGB**

Grimsby Synagogue Marriage Register 1875-1972. **JGSGB**

HULL

Finestein, I, 'The Jews of Hull between 1766 and 1880', *JHSE – Transactions*, 35 (1996–8).

IPSWICH

Coleman, A, *Ipswich Jewish Community*. **JGSGB**

LEEDS

Buckman, J, *Immigrants and the Class Struggle: The Jewish Immigrant in Leeds 1880–1914* (Manchester University Press, 1983).
The following are all private publications, available from **JGSGB**:
Freedman, M, '1891 census, Leeds: List of Jewish Residents' (1994).
——, 'Leeds Jewry: A History of its Synagogues' (1995).
——, 'Leeds Jewry: A Demographic & Sociological Profile' (1988).
——, *Leeds Jewry: The First Hundred Years* (Jewish Historical Society of England, 1992).
——, 'The Jewish Schools of Leeds 1880-1930' (2001).
——, 'Leeds Jews in the 1901 census' (2002).
——, 'Chapeltown and its Jews' (2003).
——, 'Essays on Leeds & Anglo-Jewish History & Demography' (2003).
——, '25 Characters in Leeds Jewish History' (2004).
Krausz, E, *Leeds Jewry* (Heffer, Cambridge, 1964). **JGSGB**
Skyte, H, *Care in the Jewish Community. The Story of the Leeds Jewish Welfare Board and the Leeds Jewish Housing Association (1878-1998)* (Jewish Welfare Board).

LEICESTER

Levy, S, 'Notes on the Jewry of Leicester', *JHSE – Transactions*, 5 (1902–05).
Newman, A, *Leicester Hebrew Congregation: A Centenary Record* (Leicester Hebrew Congregation Centenary Committee, 1974).

LIVERPOOL

Ettinger, P, *Hope Place, Liverpool Jewry 1836–1930* (1930). **JGSGB**
Goldman, H, *A Short History: Allerton Liverpool Hebrew Congregation* (1965). **JGSGB**
Wolfman, J, *Liverpool Jewry in the Eighteenth Century* (1987–8; in *Jewish Year Book*).

LONDON

Alderman, G, *London Jewry and London Politics 1889–1986* (Routledge, 1989). **BL**

Apple, R, *Hampstead Synagogue 1892–1967* (Vallentine Mitchell, 1967).

Barnett, A, *The Western Synagogue through two centuries 1761–1961* (Vallentine Mitchell, 1961).

Barnett, R, and Levy, A, *Bevis Marks Synagogue: An Illustrated History* (The Society of Heshaim, n.d. [1995?]).

Bevis Marks Synagogue Records, all **JGSGB**
> Part I: History of the Congregation up to 1800
> Part II: Marriages from the Earliest Times to 1837
> Part III: Marriages 1837–1901
> Part IV: Circumcision Register of Isaac & Abraham de Paiba 1715–75
> Part V: Birth Register 1767–1881, Circumcision Registers.
> Part VI: Burial Register 1733–1918

Fishman, W, *The Streets of East London* (Duckworth, 1979).

Webb, C, *An Index of London Schools and their Records*, 2nd edn (Society of Genealogists, 2000). **JGSGB**

White, J, *Rothschild Buildings - Life in an East End Tenement Block 1887–1920* (London: Pimlico 2003). **JGSGB**

MANCHESTER

Collins, L, and Bierbrier, M, *The Sephardim of Manchester; Pedigrees and Pioneers* (Shaare Hayim, the Sephardi Congregation of South Manchester, 2006).

Dobkin, M, *Tales of Manchester Jewry and Manchester in the Thirties* (Neil Richardson, 1986). **BL, UCL**

——, *More Tales of Manchester Jewry* (Neil Richardson, 1994). **BL**

Livshin, R, 'Manchester Jewry – A Guide for the Family Historian', *Shemot*, vol. 1, no. 4 (1993).

Pereira, B R, and Mendoza, J P, *History of the Manchester Congregation of Spanish & Portuguese Jews, 5633-5683 (1873-1923)* (Manchester Congregation of Spanish and Portuguese Jews, 1923). **BL**

Williams, B, *The Making of Manchester Jewry 1740-1875* (Manchester University Press, 1985). **BL, UCL**

MERTHYR TYDFIL

Bellany, W, 'A Vanished Community: Merthyr Tydfil 1830-1998', *Shemot*, vol. 9, no. 3, September 2001.

Glamorgan FHS: Monumental Inscriptions in the Jewish Cemetery, Cefn Coed y Cymmer, Merthyr Tydfil (Glamorgan FHS, 2003).

NEWCASTLE

Guttentag, G D, 'The Beginnings of the Newcastle Jewish Community', *JHSE – Transactions*, 25 (1973–5).

NORTHAMPTON
Jolles, M, *A Short History of the Jews of Northampton, 1159–1996* (privately printed, 1996). **JGSGB**
——, *The Northampton Jewish Cemetery* (privately printed, 1994). **BL, UCL**

NORWICH
Levine, H, *The Norwich Hebrew Congregation 1840-1960: A Short History* (1961). **UCL**
Lipman, V D, 'The Jews of Medieval Norwich', *JHSE – Transactions* (1967).

NOTTINGHAM
Fisher, N, *Eight Hundred Years: The Story of Nottingham's Jews* (1998). **JGSGB**

OXFORD
Lewis, D, *The Jews of Oxford* (Oxford Jewish Congregation, 1992).

PENZANCE
Brock, E, *The Jewish Community of Penzance: A Brief Account of their History*. **JGSGB**

PLYMOUTH
Green, G L, *The Royal Navy and Anglo-Jewry 1740-1820* (1989).

PORTSMOUTH
Meisels, I, 'The Jewish Congregation of Portsmouth 1766–1842', *JHSE – Transactions*, 6 (1908–10).
Newman, E, 'Portsmouth: Some New Facts about its Jewish Community', *JHSE – Transactions*, 17 (1951–2).
Roth, C, 'The Portsmouth Community and its Historical Background', *JHSE – Transactions*, 13 (1932–5).
Weinberg, A, *Portsmouth Jewry 1730-1980* (Cosham, 1986). **UCL**

READING
Krisman, S, *Portrait of a Community: Reading Synagogue 1900-2000* (2001).

SCOTLAND
Collins, K E, *Aspects of Scottish Jewry* (Glasgow Jewish Representative Council, 1987).
——, *Scotland's Jews* (Scottish Jewish Archives Centre, 1999).
——, *Go & Learn: The International Story of Jews and Medicine in Scotland* (Aberdeen University Press, 1988).

Kaplan, H, *The Gorbals Jewish Community in 1901* (Scottish Jewish Archives Centre, 2006).

SHEFFIELD

Ballin, N D, *The Golden Years of Sheffield Jewry:A Communal Diary, 1901–1945* **Cambridge University Library**
——, *The Early Days of Sheffield Jewry, 1760-1900* (1986). **UCL**
Krausz, A, *Sheffield Jewry: Commentary on a Community 1902–1980* Ramat Gan, Bar-Ilan University (British Friends, London, 1980). **UCL**

SOUTH-WEST ENGLAND

Susser, B, *The Jews of South West England* (Exeter University Press, 1993). (Mostly about Plymouth). **UCL**

STOCKPORT

Hilton, C, *The Stockport Jewish Community* (Stockport MBC Community Services Division, 1999).

STROUD

Pollins, H, 'The Jewish community of Stroud, Gloucestershire', *Jewish Journal of Sociology*, vol. 38, no. 1 (June 1996), pp. 27–44. **Southampton Library**
Torode, B, *The Hebrew Community of Cheltenham, Gloucester and Stroud* (privately printed, 1999). **JGSGB**

SUNDERLAND

Levy, A, *The History of the Sunderland Jewish Community 1755–1955* (Macdonald, 1956). **JGSGB, UCL**

TWICKENHAM

Finberg, H F, 'Jewish Residents in Twickenham in the Eighteenth Century', *JHSE –Transactions*, 16 (1945–51).

WALES

Henriques, U Q, *The Jews of South Wales* (University of Wales Press, 1993). **JGSGB**

WHITEHAVEN

Sellick, W R, *Whitehaven and Its Jews, 1774-1850* (Cumberland & Westmorland Antiquarian & Archaeological Society, 1994). **JGSGB**

WOOLWICH

Laidlaw, P, 'Jews in Early Nineteenth Century Woolwich', *Shemot*, vol. 8, no. 2 (2000).

YARMOUTH

Adler, M, 'Notes on the Jews of Yarmouth', *Jewish Chronicle*, 13 September 1895, p. 15.

Occupations

Naggar, B, *Jewish Pedlars and Hawkers, 1740–1940.* JGSGB

Rubens, A, 'Jews and the English Stage, 1667–1850', *JHSE – Transactions*, 26 (1975).

Miscellaneous

ALL AVAILABLE FROM JGSGB: FOR A FULL LIST OF BOOKS IN THE SOCIETY'S LIBRARY, PLEASE SEE THE JGSGB'S WEBSITE.

Aaron, S, *Jewish Ancestors: A Guide to Jewish Genealogy in Lithuania* (Jewish Genealogical Society of Great Britain, 2005).

Baxter, A, *In Search of your European Roots: A Complete Guide to Tracing your Ancestors in every country in Europe*, 2nd edn (Baltimore, MD: Genealogical Pub. Co., c. 1994).

Beare, A, *Jewish Ancestors: A Guide to Jewish Genealogy in Latvia and Estonia*, 2nd edn (Jewish Genealogical Society of Great Britain, 2006).

Beider, A, *A Dictionary of Jewish Surnames from the Russian Empire* (Avotaynu Inc., 1993).

——, *A Dictionary of Jewish Surnames from the Kingdom of Poland* (Avotaynu Inc. 1996).

——, *A Dictionary of Jewish Surnames from Galicia* (Avotaynu Inc., 2004).

Berger, D, *The Jewish Victorian. Genealogical Information from the Jewish Newspapers 1871–80* (Robert Boyd Publications, 1999).

——, *The Jewish Victorian. Genealogical Information from the Jewish Newspapers 1861–1870* (Robert Boyd Publications, 2004).

Black, G, *The History of the Jews' Free School, London, since 1732* (Tymsder Publishing, 1998).

Brown, V, *Celebrating the Family: Steps to Planning a Family Reunion* (Ancestry Inc., c.1999).

Cerny, J, and Elliott, W, *The Library. A Guide to the LDS (Mormon) Family History Library* (Ancestry Inc., 1988).

Fifer, S, *Jewish Ancestors: A Guide to Jewish Genealogy in Poland* (Jewish Genealogical Society of Great Britain, 2007).

Fox, C, and Issroff, S, *Jewish Memorial (Yizkor) Books in the United Kingdom: Destroyed European Communities* (Jewish Genealogical Society of Great Britain, 2006).

Frankel, W, *The Jewish Press in Great Britain, 1823–1963* (Narod Press, 1963).

Green, B, and Fulford, D G, *To Our Children's Children: Preserving Family Histories for Generations to Come* (Doubleday, 1993).

Guggenheimer, H, *Jewish Family Names and their Origins: An Etymological Dictionary* (Ktav Pub. Inc., 1992).

Jolles, M, *A Directory of Distinguished British Jews, 1830–1930* (privately printed, 1999).

Kurzweil A, *From Generation to Generation* (Harper Collins, 1994). **JGSGB**

Lewin, H, and Lewin, M, *Marriage Records of the Great Synagogue, 1791–1885* (privately printed, 2004).

Markwell, F, and Saul, P, *The Family Historian's 'Enquire Within'*, 5th edn (Federation of Family History Societies, Birmingham, 1995).

Menk, L, *A Dictionary of German-Jewish Surnames* (Avotaynu Inc., 2005).

Mokotoff, G, and Amdur Sack W, *Where Once We Walked. A Guide to Jewish Communities Destroyed in the Holocaust* (Avotaynu Inc., 1991). **JGSGB**

Pelling, G, *Beginning your Family History*, 7th edn (Federation of Family History Societies, 1998).

Renton, P, *Lost Synagogues of London* (Tymsder Publishing, 2000).

Skyte, T, and Schoenberg, R, *Jewish Ancestors: A Guide to Jewish Genealogy in Germany & Austria* (Jewish Genealogical Society of Great Britain, 2001).

Stern, M, *Tracing Your Jewish Roots* ([Cincinnati]: American Jewish Archives on the Cincinnati Campus of the Hebrew Union College-Jewish Institute of Religion, 1977).

Susser, B, *How to Read & Record a Jewish Tombstone* (Susser Press, 1995).

Wenzerul, R, *Jewish Ancestors: A Beginner's Guide to Jewish Genealogy in Great Britain*, 2nd edn (Jewish Genealogical Society of Great Britain, 2001).

——, *Genealogical Resources within the Jewish Home and Family* (Federation of Family History Societies, 2002).

——, *Jewish Ancestors: A Guide to Organising your Family History Records* (Jewish Genealogical Society of Great Britain, 2004).

——, *Jewish Ancestors: A Guide to Reading Hebrew Inscriptions and Documents* (Jewish Genealogical Society of Great Britain, 2005).

——, *Jewish Ancestors: A Guide to Jewish Genealogy in the United Kingdom* (Jewish Genealogical Society of Great Britain, 2006).

INDEX

Access to Archives (A2A) 56
Adoption 39
AJEX Jewish Military Museum 115
Aliens Registration 77
American Jewish Archives –
    Cincinnati 171
American Jewish Historical Society –
    New York 172
Anglo-German Family History
    Society 146
Archivelor Statului din Republica
    Romania 169
Archives 52
Army Chaplains 111
Association of Jewish Ex-Servicemen
    and Women (AJEX) 115
Association of Jewish Refugees (AJR)
    131
Auschwitz 125
Australian Jewish Historical Society
    152
Austrian Jewish Museum 153
Austrian National Library (Österr.
    Nationalbibliothek) 154

Belzec 126
Bergen Belsen 126
Bevis Marks Synagogue 89
Bibliography 184
Birmingham Central Library &
    Archives 69
Blue Plaques 8

Board of Deputies of British Jews
    146
Bodleian Library 70, 91
British Library 65
British Library Newspaper Library
    65, 85
British Telecom Archives (BT) 60
Buchenwald 126

Camden Local Studies and Archives
    Centre 60
Census Records 44
Center for Jewish History 172
Central Archives for the History of
    the Jewish People 164
Central State Historical Archives of
    the Ukraine – Kiev 171
Church of Jesus Christ of the Latter-
    Day Saints (Mormons) 148, 173
City of Westminster Archives 59
Civil Registration 40
College of Arms 145
Commonwealth War Graves
    Commission (CWGC) 112
Computer Viruses 105
Concentration Camps 120
Corporation of London Records
    Office 59
Council of Indian Jewry 163
Czech State Archives 158

Dachau 126

Danish Jewish Museum (Dansk Jødisk Museum) 159
Danish National Archives 158
Divorce 85

East of London Family History Society 147
Electoral Registers 50
Ellis Island 35
Ellis Island Archives 171

Family Trees 19
Federation of East European Family History Societies 172
Federation of Family History Societies (FFHS) 147
Flossenbürg 126
Friendly Societies 147

Galicia Jewish Museum – Krakow 169
General Registry Office (GRO) 84
Gentleman's Magazine 91
German War Memorial Websites 107
Greater Manchester Police Museum 77
Gross-Rosen 127
Guildhall Library 65

Hackney Archives 57
Hartley Library (Parkes Library) 72
Heraldry 142
Historisch Onderzoeksbureau Dutch Archives 162
Holocaust 120
Holocaust Centre, Beth Shalom 130
Holocaust Education Trust 124
House of the Wannsee Conference 125

Huguenot Library 66
Hull City Archives 61

Imperial War Museum 130
Institute of Heraldic and Genealogical Studies 145
International Association of Jewish Genealogical Societies (IAJGS) 90, 175
International Genealogical Index (IGI) 85, 174
Islington Local History Centre 57
Israel Genealogical Society 164
Israel State Archives 164
Italy: Genealogy of the Jews in Italy 165
Izbica 127

Jewish Brigade 109
Jewish Calendar 95
Jewish Canadian Military Museum 116
Jewish Chronicle (JC) 67, 85, 102, 148
Jewish East End Celebration Society 8
Jewish Genealogical Society of Great Britain (JGSGB) 17, 29, 66, 73, 122, 180
Jewish Genealogy in Scotland 62
Jewish Heritage Centre of Western Canada 156
Jewish Historical Museum – Amsterdam 162
Jewish Historical Society of England (JHSE) 149
Jewish Legion (Zion Mule Corps) 110
Jewish Military Union (Żydowski Związek Wojskowy ŻZW) 110
Jewish Museum – London 72
Jewish Museum – Riga 166

Jewish Museum and Library in
    Prague 128, 157
Jewish Museum Archives – Vienna
    154
Jewish Museum Berlin 160
Jewish Museum Library – Vienna
    154
Jewish Museum of Belgium 155
Jewish Names 134, 135
Jewish National and University
    Library – Jerusalem 165
Jewish War Artists 115
Jewish War Poets 114
JewishGen 28
Jews' Free School (JFS) Admission
    Registers 29

Kaunas Regional Archives 167
Kindertransport (Children's
    Transport) 132

Laminators 106
Landesarchiv Berlin 160
Latvian State Historical Archives
    166
Leo Baeck Institute – New York 160,
    173
Leopold Muller Memorial Library
    71
Libraries and Museums 64
Library and Archives Canada 156
Library of Australia 153
Lithuanian Central Civil Register
    Archives 167
Lithuanian State Historical Archives
    166
Liverpool Record Office and Local
    Studies Service 70
Lodz 56, 127
London Metropolitan Archives
    (LMA) 49, 50, 52, 99

London Museum of Jewish Life 73
London School of Economics
    Archives 58
London School of Jewish Studies
    (formerly Jews' College) 67

Maly Trostinec 128
Manchester Jewish Museum (MJM)
    74
Marriage Certificates 84
Marriage Notice Books 85
Marriage Records 44
Marriage Registers 81
Memorial Books 121
Military Badges 119
Military Records 42, 107
Minsk 128
Moving Here 29
Museum of London 73

Naczelna Dyrekcja Archiwow
    Panstwowych (Polish State
    Archives – Warsaw) 168
National Archives (TNA) 40, 49, 50,
    56, 84, 88, 112
National Archives Historical
    Manuscripts Commission
    (HMC) 150
National Archives of Australia 152
National Archives of South Africa –
    Pretoria 170
National Archives of the Republic of
    Belarus 155
National Army Museum 117
National Museum of American
    Jewish Military History 116
Naturalization Records 42
Netherlands Society for Jewish
    Genealogy 162
New Zealand Jewish Archives 168
Norwood-Ravenswood Archives 58

Ottawa Jewish Archives 156
Outward Passenger Lists from the
    UK 31
Oxford Centre for Hebrew and
    Jewish Studies 71

Palestine Brigade 110
Passport Registers 41
Photography 90, 102, 104
Poor Jews' Temporary Shelter 53
Property 100
Public Records 38

Ravensbrück 127
Reading Gravestones 92
Records of the Anglo-Jewish
    Community (LMA) 54
Relationship Chart 27
Royal Air Force Museum 118
Royal Geographical Society (RGS)
    151
Royal Mail Archive 60
Royal Naval Museum 118

Sachsenhausen 127
School Records 53
Scottish Jewish Archives Centre 62
Sephardi Records 89
Sephardic Jewish Genealogy 34, 159
Shipping Records 41
Society of Genealogists 67
Soup Kitchen for the Jewish Poor 54
South Humberside Area Archive 61
State Archive Stuttgart 160
Statny Ustredny Archiv – Slovakia
    170

Stiftung Neue Synagoge Berlin –
    Centrum Judaicum 131

Theresienstadt 128
Tower Hamlets Local History
    Archives 59
Trade Directories 50, 66

United Grand Lodge of England 74,
    149
United Kingdom National Inventory
    of War Memorials 36, 113
United States Holocaust Memorial
    Museum 124
United Synagogue 81, 89
University College Jewish Studies
    Library 68

Vilna Gaon Jewish State Museum –
    Vilnius 167
Vital Records (England & Wales) 43

War Memorials 36, 113
Wellcome Library 69
West Midlands Police Museum 74
Wiener Library 122
Wills and Administration 49

Yad Vashem Martyrs' and Heroes'
    Remembrance Authority 121,
    124, 165
YIVO Institute for Jewish Research
    174
Yizkor Books 71, 121, 123